978-0333187883
AF470612

DOLLY'S WAR

Previous books

MOTHER KNEW BEST

DOLLY'S WAR

Dorothy Scannell

M

SBN 333 18788 1

First published 1975 by
MACMILLAN LONDON LIMITED
London and Basingstoke
Associated companies in New York Dublin
Melbourne Johannesburg and Delhi

Printed in Great Britain by
A. WHEATON & COMPANY, EXETER

For my dear Chas
in our fortieth year 'at war'

CONTENTS

Chapter One
A Load of Old Rubbish 9

Chapter Two
Smashing Holiday 24

Chapter Three
To Dorothy—A House 33

Chapter Four
Just the Job 47

Chapter Five
Pregnant Pause 57

Chapter Six
Evacuees 72

Chapter Seven
The Woman from the Pru 80

Chapter Eight
The Court Martial 98

Chapter Nine
The Prescription 109

Chapter Ten
Loving Couples 122

Chapter Eleven
Homecomings 132

Chapter Twelve
Saturdays with the Cheggies 142

Chapter Thirteen
Chicken-feed 153

Chapter Fourteen
Happy Ending 161

CHAPTER ONE

A Load of Old Rubbish

'I haven't patience with you, Dolly,' said my mother. Her patience sorely tried because, visiting her a few weeks after my marriage, I had announced that I was bored, nothing exciting or interesting seemed to be happening. She knew she would have no solution for Dolly's discontent so she issued a statement which was guaranteed to pull me together, once and for all. 'Has you make your bed so you must lie on it.' She said this in tones of drama. 'It's *A*s you make your bed, Mum, not *H*as.' 'Yes,' she agreed, 'Has you make your bed.' My father looked up from his book. 'Cheer up, Dolly,' he said. 'The first forty years are the worst, so you've only got thirty-nine years and eleven months to go.'

I decided to bid my parents good-bye, for I was in a restless mood, and Mother, once having made her point, or having thought she had made her point with me, would soon be on the theme of 'Think of poor . . . and her lot,' some other unfortunate member of the family whose present plight Mother assumed would make me feel like Lady Rothschild.

I walked along East India Dock Road to Morant Street where my husband's parents lived. Ethel, my mother-in-law, was always understanding. Any trouble of mine she would always insist was 'that boy's fault', 'that boy' being my dear husband, Chas. This, of course, made me feel more loving towards *him*—think what a perfect mother-in-law she was. She, as always, was delighted to see me. I was just in time for supper, sausages and tomatoes. She told me, in her broad Suffolk brogue, of the time she was in service. The Mistress was one day discussing the lower classes, stressing that they were, in her opinion, dirty and unhygienic. This wounded my ma-in-law's pride—ever a fastidious person—

and the next morning, before taking up the breakfast sausages she licked each one all over thoroughly and watched, delightedly, while her employer's ate them with relish. 'Don't tell Charlie bor, mor,' she said. 'He wouldn't like to know I did anything like that.' Then I told her about the aristocratic master, a man with an enormous stomach, who would send for his cook every morning to give her the day's menus as he said it was his only opportunity for intercourse with her. She roared at this although it might have made my mother 'tut'.

In some strange way, domestic servants employed by people of high birth, considered themselves superior to domestic servants working for employers in trade and the like even though their wages were the same or lower. The wealth and possessions of the employers seemed hardly to have any connection with this domestic class-consciousness.

My mother's employers were not only high born, whereas Ma-in-law's were in trade, but they treated Mother like the 'lady and gentleman' they were. They addressed her as 'Leah' and even spoke of her as 'dear Leah' when mentioning her name through a third person. They *requested* a service from her and did not demand it. Ethel's mistress called her by her surname and then, according to Ethel, pronounced it wrongly purposely to impress on Ethel, her (the mistress's) superiority of class. Ma-in-law's surname was Cadge, but in a loud voice the mistress would call 'Cage'. She *ordered* things to be done. Ethel did not respect her employer, often engaging in little rebellious acts down in the kitchen to retain her 'independence'. My mother was proud of her employers. Therefore it went without saying, indeed it was never said, that my mother was more 'genteel' than Ma-in-law. Ma-in-law retained her Suffolk brogue while my mother had no trace of her Wiltshire tongue or indeed of the cockney style of speech.

Sometimes Chas's younger brother would be home when I visited his mother. I liked that, for he was great fun, a real character. He called his mum, 'Old Lady' or 'Missus'. There were, of course, no bathrooms in the little Poplar houses and Philip would stand by the kitchen sink stripped to the waist, but before commencing his ablutions he would don a hat, a straw boater in summer and a bowler-hat in winter. At one time he worked on the grocery counter of a large store. He was especially kind to old ladies and loved to make them laugh. If they were not sure which fish paste to choose he would suggest the latest which had just arrived, 'Winkle and Whale'. If they wanted something special he would say, 'Oh, just a moment, madam, I'll go down in my private lift to the basement.' He would then press an invisible push-button on his side of the counter, bend his knees and slowly 'descend', then after a little while 'up' he would rise with the required article which had been just under the counter.

'Coo,' remarked my elegant sister Amy when Mother told her of my less than ecstatic acceptance of married life, 'I wish I had my first married months over again, I had a fine time.' *She would*, of course; that went without saying. Her self-contained second-floor flat was, thanks to her adoring husband James, newly decorated, her furniture and equipment the best obtainable. It all looked so new and shining Amy never thought any housework need be done. She would rise after James had left for the office and have a leisurely style breakfast while reading the paper, clad in her honeymoon *négligée*. Then she would bath and make herself all elegant in one of her honeymoon suits and visit friends, go shopping, have a late lunch, then saunter home to get the evening meal. She was brought up sharply from this life of luxury by the woman in the flat below, a fanatically house-proud creature. She was probably jealous of Amy's way of life and one day stopped her and enquired, 'Don't you ever do any housework?' Amy said to me, really it hadn't occurred to her, but from then on, to give her her due, she changed her ways.

Although Amy and I were often, as Mother said, 'at loggerheads' with one another, yet we were never bored in each other's company, which was a compliment to me in one way, for Amy could not bear to be bored and would not suffer fools gladly. She often said she had to be dominant because she was the middle one of the family and therefore the only one without status. Since I was the ninth child out of ten I couldn't think what status *I* possessed but I envied her the doing of things 'her way' and was always mystified that the men in her life came back for more, never leaving her, as I felt they would be justified in doing by her treatment of them. James played football for a Millwall team and also the Stepney Templars before they were married. Amy used to watch but was never one hundred per cent pleased by spectatorship.

One Saturday the team travelled to Orpington in Kent for a match. Amy said they played the inmates of a mental-home! She was bored to tears and after the match Jim said, to placate her, 'Let's take a walk round the lovely Kent countryside.' Amy, knowing this would lead to courtship love-making, was too bored and now too bad-tempered for this, and while Jim was in the dressing-room changing she made her way to the station and returned home to Poplar. Dusk was falling when an agitated James arrived at our house in Grove Villas. He had been searching worriedly for Amy and was nearly frantic. He went up the main steps of the house and knocked. Amy appeared from the basement, and Jim, in his frantic state of mind and the gathering darkness, mistook her for my youngest sister Marjorie. 'Is Amy home yet, Marjorie?' he enquired. 'No,' said Amy in Marjorie's voice. 'Oh, God,' said a nearly crazy Jim, and tore off, much to Amy's satisfaction. I told Mother, who was in the scullery, and I was dispatched immediately after Jim. 'Poor chap,' said Mother. When they met it was Jim who was profuse with apologies. Small wonder that I envied my Jezebel of a sister.

Life, therefore, could not be peaceful with Amy, and one Christmas through her 'equality' with men something terrible happened in our house. My mother had been busy all day with the Christmas preparations. She was tired out and Amy was assisting her. I was in the corner of the kitchen, my head stuck in a book. My father was very late home and Mother, having cooked his tea, sirloin steak, had placed it in the oven beside the kitchen fire. Finally a tottery father appeared having celebrated the holy eve with his men friends. He sat down to this dried up looking steak, took one mouthful and throwing it on the fire said, 'What do you mean, Mother, by offering me tough steak, I could sole my bloody boots with it.'

Mother would probably have poured oil on troubled waters, but Amy, knowing how Mother had worked to the point of exhaustion for us all, said to my father, 'You ought to be ashamed of yourself, Dad, coming home and complaining when Mother has been slaving away for you all day.' Whether it was the word 'you', whether it was a daughter's criticism, whether in his befuddled mind he couldn't face the fact that what Amy had said was true, I don't know, but he got up from the table and approaching Amy in a menacing manner, he hissed, 'You cheeky little cat,' at the same time stretching out his hands as though to place them round her neck. Mother all this time was standing by the floured pastry-board smiling gently in an embarrassed way. Amy, now Sarah Bernhardt in her glory, threw up her head and seemed to place her neck into Father's outstretched hands. 'Go on then,' she said in deep dramatic tones. 'Murder me, murder me.' My father suddenly lowered his hands and said disgustedly, 'Pff, you silly little cake.' As he lowered his hands, Amy, reluctant to abandon the dramatic scene, pushed her face forward and my father's thumb caught her eye. Mother now advanced round the table and said, 'Walter, I am ashamed of you, your own daughter. How can I live with a man like that?' Again my father's befuddled pride rose strong in him. 'If you wish to go, then go,' he shouted at my mother. She had done it now, the ball was in her court, for the sake of *her* pride she *had* to go (and of course she didn't want to). 'Come, Marjorie,' she said, and she, Amy and Marjorie swept from the room.

Still paralysed in my chair by the fire I heard the upstairs front door close. My mother and sisters had not glanced at me, no invitation had been forthcoming to join them and I was left with this strange father. I could have gone with them without an invitation I knew, but to do so I would have had to pass my father and I was too frightened to do that. He turned to me and gazing hard at me said, 'And what do *you* intend to do, Dolly?' Discretion being the better part of valour (I was glad Amy couldn't hear me), I said, 'I'll stay with *you*, Dad,' feeling all the time a cowardly hypocrite. My declaration of loyal daughterly love did not seem to make him weep with fatherly tenderness or remorse, or perhaps it was *because* of my promise to stay that he said, 'Well, I'm now going out to *drown* myself!' He left by the basement door. Before I could collect my thoughts the door opened again, 'In drink,' added my father and slammed the door.

I was now alone in the house. There was no one to help me. None of my brothers and sisters was at home. David was at sea as also were Cecil and Charlie. Winifred was in Australia and Agnes, Arthur and Leonard were all married and away. I felt very lonely and very frightened. Suddenly to add to my fears I thought about the oncoming night. Suppose my father did not come back (suddenly I wished that he would), and a burglar broke in. Just as I was torturing myself with awful thoughts the kitchen door began to open slowly. 'Oh, dear,' I thought, a burglar must have been lying in wait. Perhaps he had followed my tottery father home and heard all that went on. Suddenly round the door came three faces, Mother's, Marjorie's and Amy's. All beaming, except that Amy's eye was very inflamed, all happy again. There was a knock on the door. It was Amy's James. Sarah Bernhardt once more, Amy flung herself into Jim's arms. This unusually warm welcome seemed to please him mightily. 'Oh, Jim,' she said, 'my father has tried to murder me,' copious sobs from Amy. Jim, pleased for any excuse to be close to his darling, hugged her tight. Glancing at us three and seeing our happy smiles he knew that all was well really.

My mother seemed to have enjoyed the evening in some strange fashion and slept in our room that night to let my father think she had gone. The next morning Christmas dinner was well on the way when a father with a hangover appeared downstairs. We all assumed that the demon drink would have given him an attack of amnesia, or at least remorse, but when he saw my mother wearing a paper hat and happily preparing the meal he said, 'I understood you had left me.' 'Well,' said my mother sheepishly, 'I've come back.' With a hint of dignity my father said, 'I'll allow it this time, but on any future occasion if you decide to leave let it be understood I shall expect you to be gone for good.'

I was glad Amy wasn't there for she would not like to have seen my father the moral victor. When at family gatherings over the years Amy says, 'Do you remember that Christmas when Dad tried to murder me?' the whole family, the rest of them having heard *our* story, clamp down on Amy. To make matters worse for her, James always had a soft spot for and admired my father greatly, so short of being a corpse Amy has not a leg to stand on.

I had returned from my own honeymoon just a few days before my return visit to my mother and as my old friend Edna's new house at Blackheath was a short bus-ride away from our new flat at Greenwich, on the spur of the moment I had decided to pop in to see her. Edna, possibly wanting to hear all about my honeymoon, had insisted at my wedding that she and Bill, her husband, would always be delighted to see my Chas and me. She and I were friends from my church-going days and I understood her husband had been a member of a Blackheath church choir. She was a sweet, simple, sentimental sort of creature and lived in an Elinor Glyn type of fantasy world. She was an avid reader of the daily primrose thoughts of certain newspaper ladies. Half of her tripped the light fantastic amongst the fragrant printed nothings she devoured daily, the other half of her romantic self clothed in satin, lay in imaginary abandonment on a leopard-skin rug. She had confided in me, in whispered tones, details of her honeymoon, and had just reached the exciting part where she was lying virginally on the pillows, clad in an exotic peach *négligée*. 'Bill came into the room,' went on Edna, eyes dreamily half-closed, re-living what had obviously been for her a heavenly experience. 'And when he saw me in my beautiful nightdress, he fell on his knees by the side of the bed and began to pray.' I was so surprised at this religious turn of events in what had promised to be a story of purple passion, that I was about to ask, 'What on earth could he have prayed for?' when a frantic male voice from above suddenly screamed, 'What have you done with my bloody vest?' 'Oh dear,' sighed Edna. 'He's probably slinging everything all over the bedroom. Before we were married,' she continued, 'I never dreamt Bill had this impatient streak in him.' The door of the small sitting-room burst open and a tousled red-faced man burst in, stopping short at the sight of me. 'I might as well go and sit in the car,' he said. 'There's more room in that.'

It wasn't difficult for me to see that Bill's reception of me was a little on the cool side and I kissed Edna good-bye, promising to come again to hear the next instalment of her night to remember when Bill was at work. Outside the house I waved to Bill who was sitting in a tiny car reading the evening paper. It was the sort of car which one could jokingly have said 'buttoned up at the back', but it *was* a car, it *was* Bill's, he *was buying* his house, all enormous achievements. He struggled to open the door of his car and called out politely (no doubt happy that I was departing), 'And how is dear Chas?' 'Oh, fine, just fine,' I replied. This made him glower and he wriggled back into his limousine.

Waiting at the bus-stop I pondered on the honeymoons of us working lasses. So many of us were shy of landladies, of hotel guests, and of each other, yet the romantic lady novelists of that day led us to believe that the first coming together was an effortless heavenly union, rapture with a capital R. On cloud nine all the heroes and heroines ascended, without fail, to paradise.

My sister Amy went to a hotel where the lavatory lock was faulty and on her wedding night she was trapped for a long time. Extrovert though she was she was still too shy to bang on the door or shout, while her husband, because of his bride's enforced captivity, thus reversed the normal bride and groom procedure, and arrived first in the nuptial chamber. He was too shy himself (and anyway he was not dressed for it) to go downstairs and enquire 'What kept you?' The second night of their honeymoon was wet and cold and they spent the evening in the lounge. James rose to go to bed but Amy missed the cue and he went up without her. 'Oh,' said the other guests, 'he's gone up without you tonight, my dear,' and the coy laughter made Amy so embarrassed that she sat casually in the lounge for an extra long time. Poor James must have thought he had married a bad timekeeper.

Another friend of mine who insisted that she had enjoyed a rapturous honeymoon, wept solidly through the whole of the first night. She said she had no idea why she cried but once having commenced couldn't stop and the next morning at breakfast her eyes were swollen, red and puffy and the other guests cast strange glances at her bridegroom, a charming gentle fellow. He said he felt a beast, a real Mr Hyde.

Our own flat comprised a large bay-windowed sitting-room, which looked out on to an attractive wide road of identical villas and a large bedroom overlooking the back garden; this garden went down in wide steppes to a valley. Just beyond the valley the electric trains whizzed by and because the sound of trains had been with me all my life it wasn't long before I felt the flat was 'like home'. The kitchen, bay-windowed too, overlooked the back garden and on the landing midway between kitchen and sitting-room was 'our own' bathroom and lavatory.

Being so high up I used to feel very Swiss and would not have been surprised to hear a yodeller, although I knew the performers of such two-toned singing would not be either my landlord or his wife for they were very serious people not given to intoning of any description. They were both very tall and slim. He reminded me of Mephistopheles or Punch, for he had that kind of shaped face, rather cruel-looking, and I was pleased, on the rare occasions that I saw him that he wasn't a conversationalist. His wife, who was quite pleasant, possessed a strange gait; she seemed to fall forward as though her feet were powerless.

My unmarried friends thought me very lucky in obtaining such an attractive flat so that I could be married. Indeed I felt I was lucky too, for at that time the underlying fear of maidens was the worry of being 'left on the shelf'. When a girl became engaged (and later married) there was really no need for two gloves, for these girls would wear a glove on the right hand only and carry the other glove, the left hand which bore the carats of the chosen being casually displayed on buses and trains.

'Those who go a-borrowing go a-sorrowing' had so been drummed into us by our elders that Chas and I had saved hard and gone without pleasures, indeed necessities, to purchase our home for cash. We possessed a 'walnut' bedroom suite with a 'his' and a 'her' wardrobe. The 'her' was an immense bow-fronted affair smelling permanently of varnish; my clothes seemed sadly lost and dangled limp and lonely in its vast cavernous interior. The 'his' was smaller, possessing less hanging space because it was shelved. My husband's clothes filled it to capacity so that many garments creased immediately after being carefully ironed. But it never occurred to me to let him share my enormous wasted space and it was definitely sex segregation of garments in our love-nest.

The dining-room suite of light oak had four beige leather-seated chairs and the sideboard had little squiggles on each corner (ersatz carvings really). The sideboard contained half a tea service, half a dozen cut-glass tumblers and a canteen of cutlery. This canteen, marked 'stainless' had looked lovely when it was presented to me by the staff of the London Transport office where I worked and the Superintendent had made a pretty speech saying that my fiancé's gain was the London Transport's loss. He had waved a spoon in the air and hoped we would always have time for loving, then he did the same with a fork and a knife but I could never remember what he had said about them. Sadly, however, the cutlery soon became discoloured and began to peel. Two leather armchairs and a rug from Chiesman's of Lewisham (where the gentry used to shop according to my mother) completed our home, plus of course the imitation parquet lino and the regency striped curtains. I thought the curtains lovely, setting off the high ceilinged bay-windowed room, but Chas always detested curtains and dragged them as far back from the windows as he possibly could after I had arranged them in neat folds.

I was like a new broom in my intentions to keep our home sparkling and I worked to the point of exhaustion obtaining a bright polish on the 'parquet' floor and furniture. It wasn't long before I became utterly bored with my luxurious home and my married-woman status. I suppose I was lonely, for our friends and relations lived 'over the water' in Poplar and Chas, a waiter, seemed to be permanently away working and permanently tired during the short time he spent at home. I once had a day-time visitor and I was thrilled at hearing two rings on the bell that indicated it was for me. By then my brother-in-law Philip had become a salesman and because my dear ma-in-law knew I was lonely she had asked him to call on me when he was in the district. I was delighted at the thought of a social occasion.

Philip arrived in a van which coughed hot water and

spluttered steam from an overheated radiator so I helped him lug pails of water up and down stairs to quench the thirst of his chariot. He then enquired for the daily paper with which he disappeared into the bathroom. I thought I would busy myself with preparing a nice meal for him and he would then report to ma-in-law what a wonderful cook I was and what a lucky fellow his brother was. He might also rave about the shine on floor and furniture. I knew that would please my husband's mother for she always kept a bandbox house and her cooking was superb. But the time went by and no Phil emerged from the bathroom. I kept creeping to the bathroom door and listening. From the sounds within he was having a bath! Finally he emerged, slipped on the floor, remarked, 'You want to be careful, Dorothy, polished floors can be dangerous and cause nasty accidents.' He then gulped down half a cup of tea, knocked over the jug of milk, said, 'I must dash now, I'm behind already,' and tumbled down the stairs. He shouted from the doorway, 'The Old Lady said you were lonely so I'll pop in again when I am round this way.'

As he drove away in clouds of blue smoke from his exhaust I went slowly back to survey the chaos in bathroom and kitchen. My landlady appeared at the bottom of the stairs and gave me such an odd look that I stammered, 'That was my brother-in-law.' 'Oh,' she said. 'I thought he was a strange man because his hair was soaking wet.' 'That happened in the bathroom,' I stuttered and she returned slowly to her quarters, ready, I was sure, to report to Mephistopheles that I was not the innocent young bride I appeared to be. To make matters worse my young brother-in-law had taken my newspaper with him and I had been looking forward to the highlight of the afternoon—filling in the crossword.

But there, although on the surface I appeared lonely and my relations might have thought I needed company, actually in my own home I really only wanted and felt at ease in the presence of my Charlie, and he seemed to return only to eat and sleep briefly. He had only one day off each week and the six working days were divided into short days and long days. On the long days he would leave home before ten a.m., returning home in the early hours after midnight, and on the 'short' days he would leave home at about noon and return again in those awful quiet, ghostly and unearthly hours when all good citizens were asleep in their beds. Sometimes he turned a short day into a long day in desperation at his life-style, thinking that the more money he could amass while he had his health and strength the better would be our future.

He never even had an afternoon off so I was quite excited when he told me one morning that he would be home at six-thirty p.m. We would have a rare evening meal together, just like other working people. There would be a good play on the radio, a lovely fire in the grate, and for once a mate not prostrate (with exhaustion). I went about the flat singing with joy. When it was shining to my satisfaction I went shopping. We would have a different meal, a celebration dinner. I bought an Ostend rabbit deciding to roast this with onions and mushrooms. I made asparagus soup with real asparagus. Chas was always talking about cranberries and I made a cranberry tart which looked just like the pictures in the magazines. I felt quite the county lady shopping at all the best shops; for once money was no object. We didn't drink wine, that was still for people from another world from us, so the ginger-beer rather let the side down I thought, but that too was from a good store and labelled 'home made'. I bought a jar of ginger and thick clotted cream, ever Chas's weakness. The jar was so beautiful I was longing for it to be emptied.

At six o'clock all was organised. By the time he rang the door-bell at six-thirty everything would be done to a turn. So far disaster had not struck at my culinary or other preparations, although it was a near thing when I was making a final inspection of the golden brown rabbit with the delicious smell, for I had changed into a green and gold housecoat one of my brothers had brought home from the Orient. This being a bit long I had nearly tripped over and shot the rabbit up the wall when returning it to the oven after its final basting. I thought I must remember to hold up the hem when dashing down the stairs to let my darling in.

Six-thirty came and there was no sign of a returning husband. Seven o'clock, the rabbit now looked a bit dry and shrunken. By seven-fifteen my lovely feeling of excitement had gone and I knew he must have had to give up his afternoon for some reason and carry on working. I was nearly in tears when the bell rang. Warmth flooded through me again. I was always the eternal optimist. If he sat down within five minutes the meal could be salvaged.

I opened the door to a dirty, grey-looking man with clothes torn, face cut and smeared with dried blood and a hand wrapped around with several stained handkerchiefs. 'You poor darling,'

I cried. 'Was there a train crash?' And this is where Charlie went wrong. Had the positions been reversed that question from him would have been the opening for me to come out with a dramatic excuse. But no, everlastingly honest he had to blurt out the whole story to me.

It had been his *day* off (since his days off were different each week I hadn't been suspicious, in any case I would never have dreamt my husband could be so heinously deceptive), and he had been so eager to see a special football-match that he had queued up all the morning to get in. When nearing his goal and the ticket-office the crowd had rushed the gate, he was swept off his feet and his hand was thrust through a window. He bravely sat through the match (he said he wasn't well enough to leave the ground at that stage!) and then on the stairs of the railway-station on the way home the crowd had surged forward again. Once more he was lifted off his feet and this time his clothes were torn and his head cut on a broken window. I listened stony-faced to his pitiful story. He was obviously expecting tea and sympathy from me, but my day had been ruined, all my efforts had been for nothing. He was telling me, in effect, that he preferred to spend his free time at a football-match rather than have a rare romantic interlude with me his loving bride. I was choking with fury, misery, self-pity and murderous intent, but pleased the story was told he continued more cheerfully, 'Oh, what a marvellous smell and I see that dinner is ready,' gazing at the beautiful table-cloth and flowers. 'Could you get me some water to bathe my hands and face, perhaps you could put some disinfectant in it.' I fetched the water, wondering why although I could cheerfully have stabbed him I still didn't want his wounds to become septic!

The next night he arrived home with a sheaf of beautiful tea-roses. Now these were out of season and I knew they must have cost the earth. I was already regretting the expense of the previous day, and instead of placating me Chas's extravagant gesture made me angrier still. 'However much did they cost?' I asked. This put him in a flaming mood. 'What does it matter what they cost, they're for you!' he yelled. Already regretting my enquiry I said, 'Well, if we want to save up it is stupid of you to waste money on expensive flowers.' He snatched the lovely roses from me and saying, 'I will never buy you flowers again,' dashed to the bathroom. I followed him and there he was, bashing their heads up and down on the lavatory-seat. Some days later I learnt from the wife of another waiter that an American visitor had given the roses to Chas because he had always served him so well in the restaurant and they were for 'his dear wife'. Perversely I was more furious than ever that Chas hadn't spent the earth on the flowers for me!

Before then I hadn't been aware that I had married a man with a temper, but just after the battle of the roses I was to witness it again. It was the week of the coronation of King George VI so his restaurant would not only be extra busy but have special customers from abroad. It would be a week for rich tips and Chas wanted to look specially smart and immaculate. He wore stiff white shirts with special little slits for the studs and there was a monster at our laundry who was employed just to watch for these special slits and extend them further to the edge of the shirt so that the studs would fall out and the shirt pop open at inconvenient moments, perhaps just as Chas was bending solicitously over a customer. It was my job to inspect these shirts fresh from the laundry so that there would always be one undamaged and ready for Chas to wear. Every day he reminded me of the Coronation and every day I said, 'Don't worry, I wouldn't dream of not checking your dress shirts,' but during the week of the Coronation I collected some marvellous books from the library, and books have ever been to me what alcohol is to the addict.

So I lied when I said I had checked his shirts for the great occasion, thinking of course that I would check them before *der tag.* I didn't check them that fateful week and on that important morning the laundry slasher had really gone to town like a frustrated Jack the Ripper and every shirt was ruined. 'You said you had looked at them,' screamed my husband agitatedly pacing the room in his long johns. 'You've got nothing to do all day and yet you are too lazy to do even one small thing for me.' I could have cried with guilt but I still would not admit that I had forgotten about the shirts. 'The ones I looked at are in your wardrobe,' I said mysteriously thinking that surely in his wardrobe there would be a couple of non-slashed stiff shirts. He was then, I knew, very sorry that he had accused me falsely and he tore round the bedroom whilst I stood paralysed, praying for salvation. He re-appeared like a man beserk, his teeth clenched and trembling with rage, for the time was getting on and he would be given the worst part of the floor of the restaurant if he was late, a long walk from the kitchens, the part where customers were popping in and out all the time. There was not one shirt in the house which had not been mutilated by my unseen enemy. Chas threw them all in a pile on the rug. 'Admit it, admit it, you are lying, you never looked at the shirts.' 'I must have looked at the wrong ones,' I said stupidly.

Now, more furious that he had a non-admitting wife than that he had no shirt, in his temper, he began to jump up and down, up and down on them. Relieved that he wasn't jumping up and down on me in his rage, the sight of this long-johned creature with a popping open stiff shirt and a bow tie drunkenly round his neck, started me laughing hysterically. I thought, this is why murder is committed but even though I thought each laugh would surely be my last I just couldn't stop and suddenly Chas too realised the ridiculousness of the situation and collapsed with laughter. He put a muffler round his neck and dashed off to buy a new shirt in the Strand but as he left the house in hysterics he decided to come back and tell me he was still annoyed with me. I kissed him fondly good-bye. This seemed to annoy him and he said, 'That's enough of that.'

But I felt I had worse worries than slit shirts. There was the problem of my rubbish. In those days of modern sanitation and regular refuse collections, how could I possibly worry about this, yet sometimes I wished I had been living in good King Charles's golden days where I could just have thrown everything out of the window. To get to my new silver dustbin I had to go through the kitchen of my landlord's flat, which I hated. My demoniac-looking landlord was on shift-work, so that even had I waited until his wife was out shopping before passing through their kitchen-cum-living-room to the garden, HE might have been there.

I spent hours on the stairs with my little bucket waiting for them both to be out of the house at the same time. On Chas's day off I would try to persuade him to empty the rubbish, making the excuse that I had hurt my wrist or foot. He always refused because he thought me crazy to be so inhibited and felt that the more journeys I made into the hinterland the more used I would become to entering the premises of comparative strangers. At last, as the rubbish piled up I decided I would take it down after midnight when all below would be sleeping. This was quite a job and a slow process for I had to feel my way inch by silent inch in the dark in stockinged feet. On a wet night I would have to retrace my steps and erase any muddy footprints with a dry cloth. However, all seemed to go well and I became a past master, or rather mistress, of the art of feeling my way around in the dark, but as so often happens I became over-confident.

I was on my way back from the dustbin run one night after a successful trip. I had only the passage to negotiate and then there was the blessed safety of the stairs when, with a blinding flash, on went all the lights. My heart leapt at the sudden and unexpected illumination. Facing me in the passage was an astonished Mephistopheles, clad only in a very, very short white shirt or shift-like garment. His daring apparel, on top of his unexpected appearance, paralysed my body for a moment yet my brain and pulses raced. For a moment he, too, was silently still. His nether portions were so white and so enormous he seemed to me like a half-veiled statue. I felt like a shocked lady mayoress who had pulled the cord on the unexpected. The statue came to life before the lady mayoress did and with a lightning movement Mephi's hands grabbed the ends of his shirt turning it into a leotard. This caused him to shrink from a colossus to a hunchback, as he had to crouch to secure the leotard's permanency.

'I hope I didn't wake you up,' I said brightly as I squeezed past him, scraping his bent knees on my swinging bucket. 'I just popped out to the dustbin,' and I sauntered casually up the stairs. Once inside my own quarters my nonchalance deserted me. I leant my banging head against the inside of my kitchen door. I heard voices. I just had to know what 'HE' was saying to his now wide awake wife. 'There's something bloody fishy about them two upstairs,' he was saying angrily. 'I don't believe he is a waiter, and have *you* ever heard of anyone going to the dustbin in the dark after midnight?' I wondered if he would challenge my Chas, due in at any moment, but a door closed and the downstairs lights went out. Recovering myself, I became indignant with my landlord. Surely he could not be a nice man to go to bed so scantily attired? Why my darling wouldn't even get into bed unless the top button of his pyjamas was fastened high round his neck. I wished I had been quicker-brained. I could have pretended I was sleep-walking.

Finally I hit on a solution to my problem. When I visited Mother as I did two or three times a week I took a suitcase filled with refuse. My mother was mystified, but my father simply said, 'Dolly's always been afraid of her own shadow.' I prayed that if ever I did bump into my landlord on the way out, the catches on my suitcase would not let me down.

CHAPTER TWO

Smashing Holiday

Soon after, Chas and I went to our first wedding as married people. It was a Jewish wedding and I was very much looking forward to it. I always felt thoroughly at home and enjoyed myself with friends of that faith. I admired their energy, and was fascinated by their way of speaking, their arguments, their persuasiveness and their sense of humour. The bridegroom was a shy gentle young man called Sidney. I had met him at the Toynbee Hall drama group and Norma, another goy like me, and I, had kept in touch with Sidney and his friends from time to time. He had a friend Harry, a tall beautiful young man with a vivid and attractive personality. All the girls were crazy about him he was so magnetic. Harry was to be best man. Sidney worked with his father and uncles in a workshop where the naked light-bulbs shone down on the seamstresses seated at long wooden tables. He designed dresses and could also machine and sew with the best of the girls. I thought him fantastic for I had a long struggle even to thread a needle and couldn't sew without stabbing my forefinger every time. He wore a tape-measure like a garter of honour. Harry, his handsome friend, was nicknamed 'Harry the Horse' by his compatriots and I thought he was probably a racing man interested in the turf.

Norma and I just loved the synagogue wedding, the bride so richly beautiful in a fabulous gown designed by Sidney. They dashed their wine-glasses to the floor and it was like a Hollywood movie. Norma, her husband John, and Chas and I were looking forward to the reception which we assumed would take place in a swanky hotel. Therefore it was four shocked Christians who alighted from the wedding car outside a shabby terraced house in a narrow street somewhere at the back of Spitalfields. All along the street women were sitting on wooden chairs to view the procession and I avoided Chas's surprised eyes as we entered the 'hotel'. Norma whispered to me that she needed to 'go' and I accompanied her through a passage, dingily decorated with brownish varnished wallpaper. We had to walk carefully as the floor was covered with rope mats, some square, some round, some oval, and our high heels caught in the mats proper and the edgings. We went out into a tiny back yard and were very glad we were together for round the walls of the yard were about twenty men, all wearing hats, all holding large tumblers of beer. The door of the yard lavatory had been removed and was resting against a wall in a dangerous position. Outside the lavatory, which was in full view of the 'audience', seated on a low stool was the fattest lady I had ever seen. She was surrounded by scraggy-looking chickens, all featherless and therefore dead, but otherwise intact, and she had the task of cleaning and dressing these birds under a stream of running water.

Norma and I fled back into the house. 'I shall burst,' said Norma. 'Perhaps when we've had a drink we'll be braver,' I suggested. 'I know what,' said Norma. 'When they call us for the meal we'll dash back quickly then.' 'But if that woman's got to clean those chickens and then cook them it'll be hours,' I wailed. We swallowed several glasses of wine and both felt absolutely marvellous, so marvellous in fact that we brazenly followed two beautifully gowned, furred and jewelled matrons back to the yard. At the sight of these ladies the privy counsellors disappeared and crammed themselves into the passage leaving the yard to us four ladies. The fat lady had disappeared with her factory belt of chickens leaving only a few feathers and blood-stains on the concrete to remind us she had ever been in residence there, and from a small kitchen at the side of the lavatory came the delicious smell of cooking.

At last we sat down to the wedding breakfast. One of the upper bedrooms had been emptied of all normal furniture and we sat on benches at long tables. Norma and I were literally starving as we'd eaten nothing that day, and were both a little excited having imbibed our wine on empty stomachs. Our two husbands were very quiet and very sober; they were simply longing for a nice cup of tea, which they obviously would not be getting. The meal commenced and in front of me was placed a soup bowl filled with bright yellow liquid, and lying to the side of this bright shining pond was a small round pink object. At my surprised stare Norma said, 'It's lock-chen, with one meat ball.'

I had always detested stews, clear soup and the like since I was a small child so I waited eagerly for the next course, although Chas drank his yellow stream and ate his meat ball even if he did this as though it would bite him at any moment. Came the next course, the same liquid but instead of a meat ball there was a slice of chicken breast. So delighted was I to see something I was able to eat that before all the dishes had been passed round I had gobbled down my lovely white breast and as the man on my left turned round to speak to a friend sitting on the table behind ours, intoxicated by the wine and my hunger, I rudely speared the breast from his bowl and swallowed it before he turned round. Norma was in hysterics, her husband looked astonished, whilst Chas, sitting opposite me, gazed at his penguin wife with a look of anger and hate mixed with reproachful sadness. I suppose I thought the man whose breast I had stolen would be too good-mannered to mention that something was missing, but he was no gentleman, and quite an argument ensued between him and the servers. Suddenly this breastless man turned round and said belligerently to me, 'Did you pinch my breast?' I was now so terrified I became cold sober, and my sweet Chas who normally thought that if I suffered for my own impetuous actions I would gradually reform and become a normal human being, quietly changed dishes with the man who had been robbed. At first it seemed the man would not accept the transfer even though Chas insisted his first little pink ball had 'filled him up'. Finally when the man realised that the servers would be bringing no more chicken, he ate Chas's portion. But he did this with his arm round his plate protecting his portion from me. I was so relieved that the matter had been settled, that I was full of love for my husband, but when I thanked him afterwards and apologised for my stupidity and ill-mannered behaviour he said he hadn't done it out of love or compassion for me. He could see that the man had been drinking and was on the verge of becoming violent and likely to attack me. Chas would therefore have been forced to protect me and he was apprehensive for himself for the robbed man apparently was an all-in wrestler. 'I suppose that's why he was so hungry,' I said.

After the meal we adjourned to a small room downstairs where the drinks soon flowed freely. Chas and Norma's husband were having a whispered consultation in the passage having come to the conclusion that they would be wise to collect their merry wives and depart. We said our good-byes and departed for Lyons Corner House for a nice meal. Chas, now safe, had forgiven me, and Norma and John were hysterical when they thought of the wrestler's face when he realised his breast was missing.

In the cloakroom I mentioned how attractive Harry the Horse was and wondered vaguely why he hadn't been snapped up in marriage. Norma lowered her voice. I was still a bit befuddled but eventually gathered from her non-medical language that poor Harry was a non-starter from a marriage point of view because of the abnormal size of his 'wedding regalia', hence his nickname.

Life seemed so quiet now that I was married and when Chas was away working, that I would sometimes sit in my large polish-smelling flat and try to remember the last time I had laughed at anything. It came as a shock to me to realise that I missed my previous life in a large family so much, for I had been sure that all mod. cons, nice furniture and anything I liked to eat would be the ideal existence. I was ashamed of myself for being such a scatter-brained creature that I needed spontaneous laughter to speed the days along, and although I knew the time had come for me to grow up and realise my responsibilities, that life was a serious business, I still had the urge to run back home to Mum and Dad and argue and laugh with the Cheggies again. I admitted to myself that I was a simple creature born of a simple family, but perhaps because of our childlike characters we had made a poor life into a rich one and I felt to the beatitudes should have been added, 'Blessed are the simple.' When I went home again and some of the Cheggies were visiting, without fail something would happen which would fill the old house with merriment.

One day when I arrived in Poplar, my sisters Amy, Marjorie and Agnes were already there with two of my brothers, David and Leonard, six out of Mother's ten offspring. They were sitting quietly in the kitchen with Mother, whilst Father was standing to attention in military fashion facing a severe-looking man. This man, holding a sheaf of papers in his hand was obviously a business executive and Marjorie whispered to me that he was 'seeing to Dad's pension'. The man looked round the shabby kitchen and across his face crept a look of disdainful condescension. 'I am given to understand your name is "Chegwidden",' he said. He stressed this as though being a member of the poorer fraternity my father's name should have been Smith, Brown, or White, or perhaps he should have been just a number. I think my father felt this man's superior attitude, possibly it hurt his pride as some of his 'children' were watching, and, though he was only a small man, he drew himself up to his full height and announced in the tones of the upper classes, 'Actually, Sir, my name is Walter Chenoweth-Chegwidden.' The man looked astounded, my mother's head seemed to nod from side to side with ancestral pride in her husband's revelation of his true family name, and she seemed to draw herself up too. I whispered to Amy, 'That's right, Mr Micawber, you tell him,' and the whole six of us fell into the scullery and exploded into great gusts of laughter at my father's comical stance and utterance, Mother's pride, and the deflation of the form-filling official. David always had a laugh like thunder, Marjorie like a goat and the man in the kitchen must have thought he'd entered a mad house. But of course the family name *was* Chenoweth-Chegwidden, the Chenoweth (pronounced Sheenarth by my 'swanking' father) had been dropped after my father's birth because of some disagreement Grandfather had had with that branch of the family in Cornwall.

Although my parents were always pleased to see me I had the feeling they were disappointed in me in that I *needed* to visit them so much and never wanted to pursue other social outlets. No other member of the family returned home so often as Dolly and I suppose Mother knew in her heart it was a case of having to forcibly wean me from her, otherwise I would return home for good. It wasn't that she wanted to be done with a troublesome daughter for Mum, Dad and I would be merry all the time we were together, it was that she believed they still came first in my heart and she was somehow watching Chas's interests. Sometimes when I called therefore, she would say they were going to a cinema, or to visit a relation, and I felt they wanted to go alone, without me.

Mother's gentle rejection of me took effect and I decided to go back to work. I obtained a temporary job as a shorthand-typist in the city and very quickly became close friends with the, to me, prim elderly dried-up spinster who had been secretary at the firm since the day she left school. Her name was Felicity and we were opposites in every way. She called me Dolly Dragonfly for she said I was always darting about mentally. She had some trouble with her gums and it was during the time that she was toothless and waiting for her gums to harden so that she could wear false teeth that she became engaged to the organist at her local church in Sussex. She continued to work after marriage and when her husband obtained a job as music master in London they found a flat in Chelsea. They invited Marjorie and me for the week-end, saying that as the flat possessed only one bedroom, Marjorie and I could have this and they would 'manage' in the dining-room.

We had a very nice Saturday, if a little prim and proper, for after all they were regular church-goers and all their friends were pillars of the church whereas Marjorie and I, although still believers, no longer attended church and had fallen by the wayside if not from grace. We thought in some way they were trying to reclaim us for God. At ten o'clock on Saturday night we went to bed in the bridal bedroom. How hospitable were our friends, how unselfish. These thoughts were confirmed on Sunday morning for our bride and groom appeared with two heavily laden trays, one for Marjorie and one for me; and a Sunday paper each! We both had a small pot of tea with the accompanying sugar bowl, milk and hot water, thin bread and butter and biscuits. 'Aren't they kind!' said Marjorie. 'Let's give them a surprise, let's tear through this lot, we needn't eat it all, then dash out and help with the housework and cooking.' In a flash we had gulped down a cup of tea, swallowed one slice of bread and butter, and without even opening the papers we were on our way to the dining-room.

I went first carrying my tray, but as I pushed the dining-room door it jammed on something. I put my head round the half-open door to see what was stopping it. A sight so shocking met my eyes that at first the full impact of what I had witnessed did not sink in. All I knew was that I must stop Marjorie who was pushing hard behind me saying, 'What's holding you up, Dolly?' 'Back, back,' I whispered hoarsely to Marjorie, but she seemed unable to grasp the urgency in my tone and struggled to look over my shoulder. On a narrow wooden armchair-bed was lying our hostess. Her nightdress was up round her neck. The organist, on his knees, in the nude, was deep in prayer, his face bent in reverence over his bride's prostrate form. It only needed a dog laid at her marble feet to have provided a perfect subject for a brass-rubbing. Ever so slowly the organist raised his horrified eyes to ours. Marjorie, extremely slow to take in the delicacy of any situation, murmured, half to herself, 'That's funny, I could have sworn he was clean-shaven.' Suddenly the statue let out a blood-curdling scream which galvanised us into activity. We ran back into the bedroom and slammed the door. Marjorie seemed to want to have a post mortem on the proceedings. Hardly the time or place I felt. I knew we could never face our host and hostess again. Why, oh why, hadn't we stayed in the bedroom and read the *News of the World*, which now seemed like the *Woman's Home Chat* in the light of our experience. As Marjorie said indignantly to me, '*Your* friends were married, Dolly. *I* assumed they were respectable!' I never returned to Felicity's office again.

Though I never told Chas the real reason for my leaving that firm, as our first holiday together was coming up, he was not unduly curious. As we both missed the large family I had grown up with we decided this time to go to a holiday-camp by the sea, where there would be other young marrieds.

We soon realised that a camper's life was not our cup of tea; the bright 'good morning campers', the jokes and songs *en masse* first thing in the morning left us cold and not a little embarrassed. The food, too, left much to be desired and lots of people suffered with tummy trouble. Chas was quite upset that some of the vegetables were dehydrated for to him fresh vegetables were the staff of life. He was also distressed for Lil, the lady in the next hut, sorry, 'chalet', to ours for she was becoming a nervous wreck with constipation. Each morning when he saw Lil she would, because of his specialist sympathy (I am sure she thought he was a medical student) shake her head in a negative way and then he would return to me (still lazing in bed, never one of the bright ones early in the morning) and say, 'It's *ten* days today dear, poor Lil,' so that each morning commenced on a depressing note.

He was also very cross that I won the treasure-hunt. I had overheard someone explaining the last clue and so reached the treasure first. *I* felt ashamed too, but having committed the original sin I was not brave enough to make a public confession and salved my conscience by presenting the real winner with my prize of padded coat-hangers from which was suspended a satin lavender-bag, saying I already had too many coat-hangers and lavender-bags. I thereby gained a reputation for overwhelming generosity which annoyed Chas even more.

After the first few days we did team up with some other jolly young people. Chas won the tennis prize and the table-tennis prize, fairly and squarely, of course. We joined the beach club where we met every morning for drinks and high-jinks. Chas and I were not real drinkers, he built himself up on Horlicks while I consumed gallons of coffee. One morning, however, I sampled the local home-brewed cider. I'd forgotten my mother's warning that country cider, to the uninitiated, can be as lethal as spirits and I was feeling in fine fettle, the life and soul of the party. The whole club was in hysterics, with the exception of Chas, still on Horlicks and very worried about me. I loved every moment of this rapturous experience. Someone suggested we visit the nearby town and 'have a go' on the miniature Brooklands racing-track. We all contributed to a pool for a prize for the winner.

Now we had had no experience of cars, indeed I could only ever remember having been in my wedding vehicle, but I assumed the little cars on the track were toys, like a child's pedal-car. We all selected our racers and I had to try hard to keep my eyes and ears open for the starter's instructions. 'Keep your foot on the accelerator until the bell goes,' he shouted through a megaphone. Down slammed my foot and off I shot. I was leading in no time, for by a miracle I had raced out in front without crashing into my competitors.

In the centre of the race-track was a miniature rock-garden with a pond, beautiful flowers and exotic trees with chattering monkeys climbing all over them, all this enclosed by strong mesh fencing. The crowd were cheering me on. Never had they seen such driving, the real Brooklands had come to town. I was petrified with terror, too stupid to realise that if I lifted my foot off the pedal I would slow down and come to a halt. The man had said, 'Keep your foot on,' and obediently I did. I thought I should be killed, I might even kill a fellow driver, and as I have that sort of weak nature which gives up when the going gets too rough so I began not to care if I *was* killed, although I did not want to hurt anyone else. Perhaps it was because the effects of the cider were reaching their climax, I don't know, but I could not wait for the stop bell any longer, I felt it would never ring, and as I negotiated a turn near the rock-garden, wham, with a tearing crash and an almighty flash of electricity (I had no idea the track or fence was wired up to power) I shot straight into the monkey enclosure. For one moment there was a terrible hush; every other car had stopped as though by magic. Then in the silence came the owner's shout, 'Jesus Christ Almighty,' and I knew then what a terrible thing the demon drink was. In my fuddled mind, already feverishly trying to escape from a delicate situation, I realised that I just could not emerge from the car unhurt, as indeed I miraculously was. What wrath would be poured on my head! Why I might even have to work until old age to pay for the damage. So, in my best 'Lady of the Camellias' manner I slumped dramatically across the wheel of the car.

Chas, sure I was mortally wounded, leapt from his car to come to his dying wife and tore his shin from ankle to knee on a piece of broken metal on his racer. Out of the corner of my eye I could see the blood pouring down and realised more than ever that I should have to act out my part. Since I'm no actress this would have been difficult, but the cider had made me sleepy and I closed my eyes while some strong young men, with Chas holding my hand, assisted me to a van which took us back to camp, me to bed, and Chas to the first-aid post. I had to lie in bed for a couple of hours then make a fragile appearance in the evening. 'How brave she is,' said Lil. The owner of the race-track thought I was a wonderful girl for I assured him I was 'fine' when he called, very worried that he would have to pay compensation, for he assumed the accelerator had stuck or been faulty in some way. Poor man, his race-track was out of order for a whole week and the strange thing about the whole affair, in retrospect, was the fact that Chas insisted there were no monkeys there!

CHAPTER THREE

To Dorothy—A House

It was back to Greenwich and a calmer life, I hoped, after our racing holiday. I think Chas hoped so too and we were both looking forward to the following week-end when we were to entertain my in-laws to Sunday lunch. They were all lovely people and we got on famously, so as the day drew near Chas and I were quite excited. He had the day off and helped me with the preparations. Just as my parents were opposite personalities, so were Chas's mum and dad. As a very young girl, almost a child, she had worked in a weaving-shed in her Suffolk village where the young people had a rough time with the overseer, a grim-faced woman, who would lash out at them with a piece of wood from the spinning Jenny. After her friend's teeth were knocked out by this woman, my mother-in-law, Ethel, not being adept at the spinning of the delicate silk thread, decided she would be better off in domestic service. Ethel was a woman who was never still, or so it seemed to me, never pausing in her cooking, cleaning and polishing. She cleaned her windows throughout the house inside and outside every week and I was very surprised when I saw her ironing her dusters as carefully as though they were delicate articles of lingerie. She laughed at my astonished stare and said, 'I hope you won't be such a fusspot as I have been all my life,' whereupon I confessed to her that I ironed only the collars, fronts and cuffs of her son's off-duty shirts. She thought me very clever and said I would have more time for getting on with life, that cleaning etc. is not living. She told me I would have to work on Charlie as he was over-conscientious like her and if I didn't watch him he would 'work himself' to death, which, of course, was really what my dear ma-in-law did, being unable to relax. Perhaps the mothers of those days had been brought up in too hard a school.

Alfred, my father-in-law, was as introvert as his wife was extrovert. He was so shy that he resented any intrusion of strangers into his family, and for weeks and weeks he ignored me when I first went to his house, indeed he almost sat with his back to me, but once having been accepted by him I had a friend for life. Characterwise I think he was the most marvellous man I have ever met, for his life read like a Greek tragedy, yet never once was he embittered by his suffering, always ready to help those less fortunate than himself. He was passionately fond of children and after Christmas dinner at his house he would collect from each guest money for Dr Barnardo's children's homes at Stepney, then he would put in more than he could really afford and walk with it in rain or snow to the orphans' home. He had been orphaned at an early age, the memories of his mother, Miranda, so faint in his mind that he felt he had to keep recalling them in case he should lose them in the mists of time. He always thought that he had been born in Cork but that his stepfather and stepmother had brought him to London at an early age. He was blind in one eye through—what he always said was an accident—being struck by a piece of coal thrown by his stepbrother. Before he reached his teens he was living alone in one room somewhere near the Strand and would get up at dawn to go to Covent Garden where he would buy a load of celery, clean it and trundle it across London Bridge to sell. He could neither read nor write and he bought an exercise-book, pen and ink (his most cherished possessions), and he taught himself to read and write, his head bent to the paper, the garret room lit only by a candle.

Ill luck dogged him. He worked in the kitchens of a restaurant under a glass roof which one day caved in. He flung his hands up to protect his head and the tendons were lacerated. Until he could work again he lived almost entirely on dry bread. Eventually he obtained a job in the docks, a regular job, a plum in those days, and he married a music-teacher. Within two years he had a son and a daughter. He adored his children, his wife was a gentle creature, as he was, and he felt he had come through his dark days into perpetual sunlight. But his wife died suddenly of a heart-attack when his children were both under two years of age. Eventually he married my lovely ma-in-law, and was doing quite well at work when a further blow fell.

I felt what happened has to be looked at in the context of his previous life, for he was an honest man, a proud man, a man to help anyone in trouble, but because of his days of near starvation he could not bear to waste even a stale crumb. One day when leaving the docks he saw, in the gutter, a few potatoes which really *had* 'fallen off a lorry'. To him this was wasted food and he retrieved these and put them in his pocket. He was searched at the gate and lost his job. Of course his wife was furious, why her relations in Suffolk sent them potatoes by the sack load, but of course no one who has not starved could possibly know how he felt. But in those days stealing was stealing even though the next lorry would have run over the wretched spuds.

Then followed a dreadful time for the family. He was too proud to go on relief, which was the only possible course in those days, and in the end the children were sent from school to a building opposite St Frideswide's church in Poplar where they were given free meals. My husband said it was the first time he had seen an individual steak and kidney pudding in its own tiny basin, and this miniature creation so amazed him that he wanted to take it home to his mother for he knew she would be surprised as he was. Eventually the engineer Chas's mum worked for obtained a job as a storekeeper for my disgraced father-in-law, and again, just when the family were on their feet more or less, a ship's rope caught Alfred on his blind eye and he was knocked off the quay. The bones in his feet were broken and he spent many months in Poplar hospital. Chas, then a boy, went to collect him on his discharge, his feet still in plaster, and Chas said it was the only time he had seen his father cry. At Blackwall Tunnel it was always a mad rush for buses and they had to wait ages to get one. Once the crowd had even knocked his father down when he was on crutches.

Chas's father was very frugal with himself, he would finish up the dry crusts and only ever treated himself to a weekly half-pint of beer when things were going well. This would last him all day on Sundays when he would sup it from a small wine-glass. One cigarette would last him all day too, and as they were a card-playing family, if ever he won, he would pour a fresh wine-glass of beer and treat himself to a few puffs of a Woodbine. Yet his wife was on the extravagant side and he was so pleased for his wife and children to have what they desired.

She had been a country girl and could not bear to see her house without flowers. She would take great care of them. I have even seen the last faded one, not quite dead, cherished in an egg-cup. My mother loved flowers too, but to my father these were an unnecessary extravagance. If Mother was ever in funds and purchased some mimosa or daffodils, when the temptation to pass them by was too great, we would be very cross with my father for when he came in to meals and Mother was gazing fondly at the bright promise of spring on the table he would say, 'What I want to see on the table is something with steam rising from it.'

I think my own father looked down on Alfred, my father-in-law, not only because he stayed at home and helped his wife in the house, never going to a club with MEN as my father did, but also because of his restrained drinking habits. My father told Alfred that he had brewed some good strong beer himself once but that he discontinued its manufacture because the family didn't appreciate his efforts at economy. When I told Chas's father of the home-brewed affair he couldn't stop laughing and said he was glad he was no drinker. He thought my father a wonderful man and said he was a real 'character'.

When I hear Kipling's words 'If you can meet with Triumph and Disaster', I see my father again standing in that little East End kitchen rubbing the balding top of his head, like a small boy, bewildered, sad, puzzled and then amused at the result of the failure of another of his 'do-it-yourself' projects. The 'law of averages', an expression my father was very fond of quoting, never applied to my father's experiments. They were all, without exception, disasters. To Mother's great relief I think the home-brewed beer project was my father's swan-song. At that time in my hectic pre-marital career I worked in an office in Moorgate. The staff were all middle-class (to me, blue-blooded), but in this office I was exceptionally popular. It was a charity which ran a boarding-school for the sons and daughters of impoverished clergy and the like.

One of the typists whose father was in the stockbroking business invited me to her home in Hampstead for the week-end. I had tried to refuse gracefully but Mother persuaded me to go. It was Mother's one aim in life that out of all her girls 'Dolly' should marry a tradesman. I never knew quite what she meant by a 'tradesman' and I don't think she did either. However, a real leather attaché case was borrowed from somewhere, I saved hard for silk underclothes, a nightdress and a 'ball' gown. It was the first time I had acquired silk underclothes and they were the most beautiful things I had ever possessed. The vest and cami-knickers were in eau-de-Nil crêpe de Chine edged with coffee-coloured lace. I must have made an indelible impression in these luxurious garments for my younger sister Marjorie still quotes that the sight of me in these cami-knickers at the dress rehearsal was the most beautiful sight she has ever seen. The trouble was that despite that compliment I didn't possess a face to match my figure and since I could not walk about in the City of London clad only in my cami-knickers I was still a 'nice homely girl' because I possessed such a matronly face.

However, with great pride, Mother packed my week-end case and I can see, even now, her work-worn fingers gently stroking the elegant silk in its tissue-paper. Mother had to pack the case on Thursday evening because she was visiting the miniature village at Beaconsfield with the Mothers' Union on Friday, and as I had to be up early on Saturday morning she was afraid 'slap-dash Dolly' would forget something as I had to bathe and shampoo my hair on Friday evening. My case was closed, but left unlocked on the kitchen dresser, awaiting my ascent into society.

Friday was a Borough holiday, so my father, a plumber with the local council, had the day off. This perturbed no one at the time although, with hindsight, it should have done, and when I left for the office on that fateful Thursday he was up, washed and shaved, with an excited look in his eyes and prancing almost boyishly on his feet. He seemed anxious for us to depart, me to work, Mother to the church to meet her friends and the coach. Father actually stood at the gate waving us off, a thing I had never known him do before, and the love-light shone in Mother's eyes. 'Not many men would be so unselfish as to wish their wives a happy day when they have to be alone all day and prepare their own meals,' she said proudly. I was surprised at Father's eagerness for Mother to enjoy the outing but I felt stirrings of guilt at my suspicious thoughts as I watched her greet some other poor old mums, all as excited as children. I forgot my apprehension about the week-end and also my suspicions of my father's reformed behaviour and sat on the tram thinking only of my green silk cami-knickers and my 'chiffon' lisle stockings. The stockings had cost the exorbitant sum of 1*s.* 3*d.* In my mind I was *Lady* Dorothy.

Eight hours later my 'eau-de-Nil' dreams were shattered. I arrived home to find the kitchen in a turmoil and Mother flushed and terribly worried. Father was flushed too but as excited as he had been in the morning, almost delirious, and talking in half-sentences. Mother said, 'I'm sorry, Dolly, I've got them soaking in cold salt water in the kitchen sink.' In the bowl in the sink was a sort of wadge of brown material with, here and there, a green spot, like little pieces of specked apple. I gazed at these bright green spots and the penny dropped! This brown wet mass was my society undies. Apparently Mother had arrived home soaked through because of a freak storm (comforted by the thought of a welcoming father and a singing kettle), to find the kitchen in a dreadful mess with a tottery and victorious father waving his hands round the kitchen at assorted sized bottles of strange-smelling brown liquid. Someone had given him an ancient recipe for home-made beer and Father said it was 'true elixir'. Mother looking at the soggy brown material on the table had asked, 'Whatever did you strain it through?' 'Oh,' said Father, 'I was lucky there, in the case on the dresser I found something that was "just the job".'

Of course I cried; Mother, tired out, nearly cried too and as the rest of the family appeared from work Father sunk further into disgrace. But still he had the end results of his zeal which kept him above the water-line of shame. He placed all the bottles carefully and lovingly on a shelf in the coal-cellar, the door of which led into the kitchen, although the cellar was half under the front garden. Every bottle exploded, without exception, but with true poetic justice they did not explode *en masse*, but one each day. Mother was terrified to go into the cellar until the last one had been blown to infinity.

I went for my upper class week-end in my ordinary undies and distinguished myself by slipping on the highly polished parquet floor and putting my elbow through a glass pane in my hostess's china cabinet. I felt miles removed from the elegant young men at the ball in their dinner suits (in any case they couldn't dance nearly as well as the boys at Poplar Town Hall with their 'coming rahnd') and the little cardboard 'programme' with its tiny silver-topped pencil and tassel in which my dances were to be reserved was sparsely filled with duty invitations from my office friends' brothers. I knew then that even my green silk cami-knickers would not have prevented me from being a foreigner in a foreign land and I made up my mind to buy my father an ounce of his favourite tobacco when I returned home. How could I blame him, he could never have seen green silk undies in his life before. His rememberings would only have been flannel or winceyette.

My mother and my father-in-law really liked each other. He brought out the maternal in my mother and she made a great fuss of him, seeing that he had exactly what he was fond of at mealtimes. They both shared the same gentle traits and an intense love of children. On the momentous day of my in-laws' first visit to Greenwich, Chas's parents brought along his elder brother Robin, with his wife Olive and their small son Geoffrey, together with Annetta, Chas's sister, her husband James and their son, also named James. Now the boys, James and Geoffrey, were two live eels, for ever active, never still, and whilst the adults played cards the boys dashed from room to room and up and down the lino-covered stairs until it was time for them to leave. Everyone kept saying they had spent a really happy day and Chas and I retired to bed pleased with the success of their visit.

The next morning, on the stairs, was a sealed envelope addressed to 'The occupant of the upstairs flat'. I was mystified, for as the envelope was unstamped, I couldn't think from whence it came and how it got on to the stairs. I stood by whilst Chas opened the envelope. 'Sir,' it began, 'Accept one week's notice to leave the premises, as from today.' We sat down silently until Chas said, 'Sir,' 'Sir,' 'Sir,' in different tones as though he was practising with a Shakespearean company. This word 'Sir' seemed to shock, absorb, and worry Chas more than the ultimatum itself. Apparently Mephistopheles had been unable to sleep on Sunday because of the noise made by Chas's nephews, yet only the week before Mrs Mephi had said our presence in the upstairs flat was a delight. As she added, 'We never hear a sound from you,' I thought at the time she meant 'absence' and not 'presence'.

However, Robin came to our speedy assistance, not because dear little Geoffrey had been half the cause of our summary dismissal, but because he was having trouble with rather eccentric neighbours. Rob was buying a house on one of the new estates which seemed to be mushrooming everywhere in 1937. He had become friendly with the people next door but after a time began to miss some article from his house, always a day or so after the visit of these new-found friends. Once it was a solid silver sugar-bowl, the next time, the silver tongs which 'went' with the bowl, and then a piece of porcelain from his china-cabinet. He still didn't suspect his neighbours until one evening he and Olive were invited next door to play cards and lo and behold on the sideboard were Rob's missing articles. The neighbours seeing the amazed stares of their 'benefactors' said, 'Oh, you are admiring our little bits and pieces. We collect them you know, and we have had these pieces for many years now.' Rob was speechless and helpless, hardly believing what he had seen and heard, almost hypnotised by the neighbours' calm manner into believing that by some coincidence the neighbours possessed identical articles to his own and that his had been stolen in some other mysterious fashion. But Olive, more a woman of the world than Rob, began quietly to plot a campaign to recover her treasures.

In the midst of this plotting other mysterious happenings took place next door. The man was never at work and, having obtained a gun from somewhere he would spend all day long fashioning a bullet for it, then he would dash into the garden and fire this bullet up into the air. He 'found' a stopwatch and every morning he would stand at his bedroom window, curtains drawn back, and time all his neighbours on their way to the city.

All this would have terrified me, but Olive became dangerously calm. She was determined to recover her stolen goods. It was in the midst of her campaign that we received notice to leave our flat, so we four clubbed together and bought a house at Forest Gate. The last I heard of Olive's eccentric neighbour was a report that he was in hospital. He had taken to walking about his house, clad only in a shift, in full view of the passing populace (being English though, the neighbours simply sailed past with their heads averted) and whilst following one of his favourite pastimes, that of amorously chasing his yelling wife, a heavy door had slammed on him with disastrous consequences. His absence from home whilst at the casualty department of the local hospital was Olive's long-sought-after opportunity to recover her possessions.

The purchase of our house at Forest Gate was the speediest legal transaction ever known. We were the first customers at a new building society which had opened at Stratford. The owner's solicitor acted for both sides in the transaction and Olive and I never saw him for the deal was concluded between Chas, Rob and the solicitor at the buffet counter at Liverpool Street station. They were told the solicitor would be there waving a red spotted handkerchief, and money and deeds were passed over in a surreptitious Fanny-by-Gaslight manner. My father, and also Chas's father were very worried about it all and for some time Olive and I wouldn't have been surprised if some mysterious caller had visited us with the statement that we were trespassers, especially as Chas said the solicitor looked like a ghost, very thin with sunken eyes, a bald skull-like pate, and a sepulchral voice. I am glad Chas went to this legal appointment instead of me for it had almost been decided that I would be, with Rob, the joint owner of the house as Chas couldn't always get time off from his restaurant to carry on the negotiations.

Then my mother would have been worried for, confusing the issue slightly, she always felt because I trusted 'strangers' I might one day be the victim of the 'white slave traffic'. When I dismissed her fears as utter stupidity my father would wink and say, 'Those old Sultans would give a lot of money for a girl with white skin like yours,' then he would add, 'They'd make you keep a veil over your face, of course.' This always sent my brother David off into his thunder-like laugh, and I would flinch and ponder how my parents had not only kept their sanity but also their sense of humour with ten noisy lively offspring. My father always seemed to be trying to relax in his home-made barrel chair, my mother quietly sewing by his side. I often thought they should, like two little fairies, creep away from the noisy scenes they had so innocently created. They never complained of our noise, indeed my father thought all men should live their own lives and indeed he criticised no man (politicians excepted, and then only their policies, not their way of life). My mother was proud of her large family and possibly did not see it as the noisy writhing mass of which I was part. My father probably kept sane by having the gift of being able to stand aloof from it all and live his own life. I think the size of his family shocked him, I felt he suspected he had been 'conned' by love in some way. Love in the shape of Mother and in some secret way he 'blamed' her for his 'surrender'. Yet Mother with her calm grey eyes would look any man in the eye without that secret 'come hither' look that a willing male could recognise. I often wondered if his home-made truss, which Mother obstinately insisted 'Dad didn't need', was not a symbolic chastity-belt, a monk's-hood of his own weaving. Ten children were enough.

Our time at Forest Gate was to be a brief sojourn, although at the time of our holiday in Jersey, with Rob and Olive, we were unaware of the forthcoming break-up of our happy foursome. We were very excited because it was our first trip abroad. Well, for three of us; Chas had spent a marvellous holiday in Germany with the Rover Scouts of Poplar before we were married and before I knew him. It had been the holiday of his life, the warm welcome of the German people, appetising food, and he would tell me of the beauty of the Hartz mountains where he had met a very strange man who had insisted on telling Chas all about a man named Hitler who would change many lives, including Chas's! I think this man frightened Chas who thought him crazy.

The crossing to Jersey was extremely rough. I loved this and stayed on deck revelling in the stormy sea while the rest of the party turned green and retired to a cabin. However, we had a lovely hotel at St Helier with superb food. There were lots of other young couples there and Olive and I looked forward to a happy social time, but Chas and Rob made friends with two elderly bachelors from Bow. They were 'Brothers of Elim' and wore badges to prove it. I think they had been tram-drivers, but were now retired. They were very happy to be with us but insisted on calling Olive and me 'the females'. So it was, 'Perhaps the females would like a picnic?' or 'What do the females feel?' and 'I am sure the females would like to share the last tomato.' They wore dark suits with waistcoats over their pullovers, even though there was a heatwave on at the time, with white plimsolls, and they wore their hair like the singing barbers in the old American beer-halls, parted in the middle, with shiny waxed quiffs laying athwart their foreheads like varnished oyster-shells. Olive and I thought them very dull indeed and gazed enviously at the other young couples who had joined into jolly sociable crowds and whirled every night round the dance-floor. Our Brothers of Elim probably thought dancing and drinking the pleasures of the devil; we could tell that by the way they said 'females'.

That was until the night the Brothers decided to repay 'our' kindness by inviting us to their room for a 'little' drink. My dear husband rarely imbibed but the Brothers had obtained so many and varied bottles of the demon drink that Chas really fell in love with the champagne (later insisting he had only been 'polite'), and when we left the Brothers' room in the early hours of the morning we all felt very strange indeed. Chas had really had one over the eight. He had lost our room key on the way. It was too late, or too early, to wake up the hotel staff and Olive said we should have to share their room. Rob had already fallen into bed, and we thought, a deep coma. Olive suggested she and I creep into the bottom of the bed and Chas could take Olive's normal place next to Rob. This we did with much giggling, but when the light was out, up jumped Rob. Switching on the light he glared furiously at Chas and shouted in a dramatic voice, 'What man dares invade my marital couch?' He then pulled the clothes off Chas and shouted, 'Out, out, out.' This woke little Geoffrey (I had already fallen out of Rob's bed with fright at his Shakespearean act), who looked delighted and said, 'Oh, goody, Uncle Charlie has come to play with me.' Olive, realising that Rob was, to say the least of it, getting very bad-tempered, his jolly party feeling having suddenly left him, grabbed little Geoffrey, snuggled down with him next to Rob and switched off the light. This sudden quiet and darkness was quite frightening; the room was strange and I was afraid whilst feeling about for Geoffrey's bed, which Chas and I would have to try to share, I might start getting into Rob's bed and goodness knows what he would do then. His attitude had been one of outraged dignity and anger at our presence, as though we were invading enemies, not his dear relatives needing a place to rest our heads.

A sudden groan from the corner of the room guided me to my couch for the night. My eyes, now a little used to the darkness, made out a nude figure on this single bed. Good grief, Chas was lying flat on the bed, arms and legs stretched out, he had not even left six inches of space anywhere into which I could crawl until dawn broke. First I tried to get his singlet on but he seemed so heavy and stiff that I couldn't even get it over his head and each time I tried unearthly groaning emanated from him. I searched around on the floor in the dark to find the covers but each time I threw these over him he cast them off. I knelt by his bed for ages, trying to keep him covered for I was so worried for Olive in the morning. It might spoil her holiday had she viewed my husband not only in his birthday-suit but in so very abandoned a posture. I crouched on the floor replacing the covers like an automaton; my head ached, I felt sick, and a deadly hatred for my spouse overcame me. Three human beings were snoring away in that room; I had drunk less than any of them and I felt more than hardly done by. Chas always led people to believe he was the business-like partner, me irresponsible and even scatter-brained, always losing important documents and the like, yet *he* had lost our key, *he* had put me in this embarrassing situation with his brother. If I could have noiselessly punched my darling I would have done so willingly and enjoyably, but he even groaned like a cow in labour when I threw the covers lightly over him. Suddenly he moved his position and I squeezed into the few inches of space on the edge of the bed, intending to stay awake so that Olive's first morning glance would be at two shrouded figures.

But, as so often happened with me, a few hours after a good intention has been sincerely promised, all memory of it becomes erased from my mind, and I awoke to blazing sunshine and the sight of a yellow dragon on a blue silk cloth. Olive had woken at the maid's knocking with the morning tea, forgotten, for a moment, all the events of the preceding night and glancing at Geoffrey's bed nearly froze with shock for Chas and I were lying two nude abandoned figures, my petticoat having in some mysterious way transformed itself into a neck scarf. Olive had scrambled out of bed, thrown on her Japanese kimono and was holding her arms in their wide sleeves stretched out in a yawn above us as the maid came in. I dressed a dazed and headachey Chas and as I put his jacket round his shoulders, out fell the key to our room!

Olive was the most marvellous person to have around at times of crises. She was dark, slim, agile, and calm, and it was difficult sometimes to know what she felt or thought because, an entirely opposite character to me, she didn't wear her heart on her sleeve. What we had in common was a sense of humour. Like me she didn't laugh out loud, or long, or much, but the same funny situation would strike us both instantly, and her funny little squeak in the throat would amuse me too. She was very tolerant of the rest of us on that holiday for not only had she helped over Chas's night of inebriation, but at his apology had insisted she had noticed nothing untoward in his behaviour or demeanour, so that knowing she was looking forward so much to the weekly fancy-dress dances at the hotel, we really ought to have been more co-operative about it.

Oh yes, we all decided we would enter; not only were the prizes marvellous but there was a special prize for the entrant whose identity remained a mystery to the rest of the guests. Robin, intellectual and serious, wanted a dignified costume to match his character. Because I was plain and homely I wanted a glamorous costume and, much to Chas's disgust, I was eager for a tutu or a slave costume with split georgette trouser-legs, lots of bangles, a bare midriff and golden brassière separated in two. Chas, who was shy about the whole affair, would have been quite happy in his waiter's uniform. By the time we had all made our choice all the glamorous costumes had gone from the fancy-dress shop. Rob refused any of the ordinary ones left and Chas felt it a good opportunity to stay in civvies as company for Rob. I refused to go as a witch or Dick Whittington and Olive casually chose my rejected Dick. We all told her she was wasting her time but she just smiled.

It was a marvellous party with many fabulous costumes and 'Ghandi' was there, mystifying everyone. All the evening before the parade people were trying to guess the identity of the little dark man who looked so much like Ghandi. It was uncanny.

Several people, after many drinks, insisted it *was* Ghandi himself. We assumed Olive had thought better of going in for the parade for just before it started she was missing, but towards the end of the march past came Dick Whittington and his cat. A real live cat was following Olive at her heels, he never left her, and the applause was so great she won first prize. She told us her secret afterwards. She had obtained a fish which she wrapped up in her Dick Whittington bundle, shown it to the hotel cat, then kept her bundle on the stick within a few feet of his nose.

Little Geoffrey won the prize for guessing the mystery man, much to the mystery guest's annoyance. Rob had gone upstairs and as Geoffrey had been awake had brought him down to see the parade. On catching sight of Ghandi, Geoffrey had yelled, 'Hallo, Mr Pyjama Man.' Mr Pyjama Man was Geoffrey's name for one of the guests to whom he had taken a fancy. He would say good morning to this young man and his wife and had given him this nickname because of his club blazer which was pale and striped. The young man had shaved his head and his wife, an actress, had made him up professionally and had absented herself from the ballroom so that she wouldn't be seen husbandless which might have given the game away. She was annoyed too, because she had been boasting that as an experienced actress, with make-up, she could disguise anyone.

The following week, Olive, fired by her success as Dick, went as a pirate, with bare legs and feet, torn tight breeches, scarred face (with amateur make-up) and a knife between her teeth. With her slim boyish figure, her agility with such marvellous piratical leaps, no one guessed her identity. This was really heaping coals of fire on the heads of Mr Pyjama Man and his wife who for the rest of our stay were a little cool and distant, although little Geoffrey seemed not to notice and always bade them a cheery 'Good morning'. The trouble was that he was absolutely fascinated, having discovered that Ghandi was toothless and was always requesting his friend to 'do it again and have just gums'.

Sadly, however, I went down with sunstroke and got ticked off by the doctor, but since I had spent the holiday wrapped up like a cocoon out of the sun as my red hair made me prone to sunstroke, I thought him extremely unfair.

On our return from Jersey, Rob's firm offered him a grocery business, on which they had been losing money, and Rob, feeling he and Olive could make something of this opportunity, accepted, and soon after our return they left Forest Gate. They worked, indeed slaved, in this business and the following Christmas we went to stay with them. On the Christmas tree was an envelope addressed to 'Charlie and Dorothy'. It was a gift to us of their half of the house at Forest Gate!

CHAPTER FOUR

Just the Job

My youngest sister, Marjorie, my mother's tenth and youngest child, was now to be married to her Alfred. They had been busy searching for a flat so that although we were sad when Chas's family moved, it meant there was an empty flat for Marjorie at Forest Gate. Everything went so smoothly for her wedding that I was a little envious and she looked so pretty too in her white classical gown with four bridesmaids in diaphanous spring green. I wore a dark purple suit with a grey crêpe-de-Chine blouse which had stitched collars and cuffs and in a Jewish hat shop in the Mile End Road they made me a little grey hat the same colour as the blouse. They really were clever those Jewish hat-designers, for not having a 'hat-face' I had never possessed a hat which looked even passable, but this one really did do something for me. Enhancement was too mild a word for this miracle, and the grey with the purple suited my auburn colouring. I knew I looked really stunning for on my arrival at the church my fashion-plate sister, Amy, eyed me up and down and announced, 'The suit's too small for you, Dolly, but I will buy it from you.' In a warm sisterly mood I said, half-believing that my figure 'showed' too much, 'Thanks, I'll let you have it,' which I did, but with her dark skin somehow it never really looked anything again but an ordinary suit. But it was my own fault for not believing the rest of the family when they said, 'Dolly, you look marvellous.'

The reception was held in the Institute of All Saints Church and we had dancing and games and Marjorie's wedding was voted 'the wedding' of the family. Certainly I enjoyed it much better than any of the other weddings we had had, including my own. Secretly I wished Marjorie a smoother honeymoon than

I had experienced and she came back brown and happy but confided in me that her honeymoon night was a little frightening for she thought she had been 'wounded' and her panic scared her bridegroom so much he lit his pipe to try to keep calm, but somehow got the bowl of the pipe upside down and set fire to the bedroom carpet.

Since the disaster of my own honeymoon we had decided that birth control was not for us, we were not clever enough to manage this scientific non-arrival paraphernalia, and had philosophically decided to let nature take its course. Well nature had decided to laugh at us for no babies wanted to be parented by Chas and Dorothy. I was a little miserable about this for I began to look at all the lovely babies in their prams and wonder what ours would be like if ever we were fortunate enough to manage such a miracle. At the same time I felt that I wouldn't like my baby's father to be a waiter and work for such long and arduous hours. I tackled Chas about this and he said of course he would like another job, but was terrified of being unemployed and in any case jobs were still difficult to obtain in the late 1930s. I thought he had no adventure in his soul and although I nagged him about it constantly it did no good. Therefore I began to scheme for the future, and decided if jobs were scarce in shipping, for which Chas had the necessary qualifications, I must think further afield for another 'respectable' job. One evening the Prudential agent called with the District Manager canvassing for business and I enquired as to the prospects of an agent's position. 'Oh,' said the District Manager, looking at Chas's occupation on the new endowment form, 'waiter'. 'Our agents have to have a good education, a smart appearance, be clever with figures, and be able to sell insurance and advise people about savings.' Because he had touched my pride on the raw, over-sensitive I assumed that a waiter was not considered a man of education. I wrote to the Prudential, in my best handwriting, and signed the letter 'Charles W. Scannell'. I said nothing to Chas for I knew it would worry him, and then THE FORMS came. I filled them in with beautiful printing and writing, telling a few white lies as to education and I believe I made him a supervisor at his restaurant. A week later came an epistle inviting Chas to an interview and a written examination. If he was accepted, then a stringent medical examination would follow.

I wandered about all the evening searching for suitable words with which to break the news to my darling, but when he came in I blurted it all out. He was horrified at what I had done, he made me feel I had forged Bank of England documents, but at last I convinced him that what mattered was the fact that even if he'd had no education he was still as knowledgeable as many a more educated man and he did know how quick with figures he was. A more determined character than he, I used threats as to what I would do if he didn't attend for the interview and examination. Finally he went, looking a little under the weather. I hadn't told him all the lies I had written on the form for he just would not have gone for the interview, and I kept my fingers crossed that my answers to the questions on the forms would not be challenged. I felt worried for Chas and also myself. He would come home like a raging lion if a pertinent question was asked, for my husband was of that rare breed of husband—he was physically unable to tell a lie, even a little white one, indeed he couldn't even embroider a joke, everything had to be the absolute truth for an untruth would almost choke him. I suppose that is why he rarely told a joke, for who wants to listen to a funny story related almost as a vicar announces a hymn.

Always the eternal optimist I was sure he would pass the interview and written examination and be sent on in the afternoon to the medical officer. Although he was one hundred per cent fit, at that time an exceptionally thin man was medically suspect, and I thought I would help him through the physical examination. I filled his pockets with bags of pennies and said he could absent-mindedly put his overcoat over his arm when stepping on the scales.

All day long I wandered from room to room. The house was quiet for Marjorie had gone back to work after her marriage, and finally when dusk was falling in came 'The man from the Pru' for he had passed the interview, written examination and medical examination with flying colours. Well, perhaps it isn't quite true to say he had passed the medical with flying colours for the doctor had discovered my ruse with the coppers, but he said to Chas, 'Give my good wishes to your dear wife and tell her you are quite healthy, *for a skeleton*' and then he had added, wearily, 'What does it matter, the war will be on us soon and we might all be gone.' With these cheerful words he passed my husband A.1.

Everyone was delighted that Chas, now a Prudential agent, was released from his slavery of waiting on other people. He soon became such a conscientious and successful agent that it was a mystery to me how he ever worked as a waiter in the first place. How soon I forgot the depression of the thirties, the dole queues, men with better qualifications than his, unemployed, I even forgot how pleased we were that through being a waiter he was able to support a wife, for he would have remained an 'ancient' junior had he stayed with the firm he started to work for on leaving school because promotion there went to 'friends' of the management.

Chas was slight and short and hardly reached up to the office counter when he first began his city career and was very proud that one of his jobs, the one with such power, was the drawing of the BLUE line across the page of the staff signing in book. This blue line was drawn across the page at 9.15 a.m. and every morning Chas, a real little Hitler, would eagerly watch the clock and at the precise second, like the sword of Damocles, inevitably and irrevocably draw the thin blue line. It mattered not that through the glass doors a tearful typist or an irate clerk could be seen approaching. Chas drew his blue line with delight. Then he handed out the late excuse slips—'I was . . . late this morning because . . .' and the excuses were ingenious and varied, with the exception of the late slip which an old stalwart of the firm received every morning during the two years Chas wielded power over *tempus fugit.* Come rain or shine, summer, spring or fall, the old stalwart's excuse was the same, a grand thumb to the nose gesture to authority— . . . because of FOG. Chas is so ashamed of himself and his conscience troubles him now when he recalls his joyful period as guardian of the time-keeping book.

Chas's insurance round was at Dagenham, rows and rows of identical houses, long roads of sameness. He was extremely popular with those friendly people, not because he was a jolly sort of caller, but because there was nothing he would not do for them, he was trusted and respected. I knew he would make an excellent agent but later on when I took over his round during the war even I was surprised at the esteem in which he was held and touched by the way he had helped people far beyond the line of duty.

My mother was very pleased that Chas and I were beginning to rise in the world, class-wise, or at least she felt we had taken our first few faltering steps towards the life of a 'tradesman' and his consort. She had never really been 100% for my marriage with Chas for, although she liked him, because of his lack of flesh she was quite convinced my life would be one of attendance on an invalid and her unspoken belief was, I was sure, 'Dolly will soon get fed up with that.' She seemed to me to be always watching my husband with a look of maternal sympathy, feeling that should he ever be confined to a wheel-chair it would not be long before the said wheel-chair and its delicate contents would either be under a bus or over a cliff provided that my invalid, as a non-earner, would ever have been able to get to the sea. She adjured him to 'wrap up well and keep well shod' in the treacherous winter weather we seemed to experience then, although she thought the outdoor life might set him up if Dolly kept him well fed with good home-cooking. The trouble here was finance, for now that Chas was a white-collared 'gentleman caller' this commodity was an intensely scarce one. His basic weekly wage was £3, our last £50 capital was deposited as a sort of indemnity, and Chas had to contract a life insurance with the company, so that after weekly deductions and rent of 22*s.* 6*d.* per week, there was about thirty shillings left for all other necessities, including food.

In addition to this 'struggle', possibly because I had completely forgotten my intense desire for a baby, I became pregnant. This meant the procuring of baby clothes, cot and pram. It was, of course, the immediate future which was a bit desperate money-wise, in the long term the prospects were rosy for not only would there be commission on new business but there were half-yearly, or yearly, lump sum payments for the handling of national health insurance. I loved writing the cards which I did in my best writing and printing, watched over by the eagle eye of Chas, ever confident, as he thought me scatter-brained, that I would either lose a reference card, or put one in the wrong file.

The problem with keeping one's head above water knowing that solvency was just around the corner, was that one's stock of clothes and appurtenances always wanted renewing when the lump sums did come; therefore, like a vicious circle, we would again be waiting for the next 'windfall'. We had never had many clothes being of a saving nature. True, this had enabled us to supply the £50 deposit needed for the job and prior to that the deposit for the house at Forest Gate but at one time during my pregnancy I was walking about with cardboard in the soles of my 'holey' shoes which brought back the memory of my school-friend Lizzie who was once so excited at finding 'a luverly bit of cardboard for me shoes, look Dolly, it ain't even cracked'. I don't know whether my family would have rallied round had they known of our temporary set-back. They really all had a hard job to keep their heads above water, as most people had in the thirties, and in any case we had always been a most independent family and had told no one of our money troubles. Chas's father knew of our plight and wanted so much to help but he had scrimped and saved and gone without to amass the small amount necessary for a deposit on Chas's sister Netta's house when, with a small baby, she was without accommodation. Chas felt we really couldn't borrow the money which Netta was paying back to her father weekly, although his dear father was pressing him to do so. No, independence was the watchword of all us young-marrieds and teenagers in those far-off days. Chas's brother Phil, always so generous and always the dandy where clothes were concerned, presented Chas with a pearl-grey suit, which we had dyed dark brown but tragedy stalked there, for nursing a friend's baby one day, the baby had an 'accident' and the lovely dark brown suit became pearl-grey again round the crutch.

To make matters worse we had to leave Forest Gate and live nearer Chas's agency at Dagenham and since the area was a mixture of new-town council-houses, for which we weren't eligible, and estates of newly-built private houses, it was difficult to get accommodation. Oh, those various 'stays' in odd furnished rooms, washing up on the table, cooking over a gas-ring or fire. I was getting larger and unhappier each day and frantic that we wouldn't get settled before our baby was born. At last our luck turned and one of the other Pru gentlemen found us a lovely flat in a lovely road at Ilford. He informed us that the owner-occupier was a widow, a most charming woman, an absolute darling, so the fact that we had to share her bathroom and kitchen would be no problem at all. Well, he was so right, she was a real charmer, an absolute angel to everyone, including Chas, especially Chas, but within minutes of our occupancy I felt 'someone walking over my grave' for when this charmer gazed at me with her glittering eyes, so dark they looked black, I knew that she hated me with a deadly hatred. Some deep native instinct from time immemorial gave me a feeling of cold and sickly fear.

It is always difficult to be in the minority of one. Later on when this lady behaved so malignantly to me when I was alone, any reports on her behaviour to Chas or my family were taken as strange imaginings and a peculiarity of my condition. 'Oh, you're not used to living with strangers,' my family would say. 'Just do all you can to please Mrs . . .' From Chas it would be, 'You do let your imagination run riot with you,' and he would add, 'I find her exceptionally charming and helpful.' I was so afraid of this woman in the lonely evenings when Chas was out canvassing I used to imagine that she wanted me gone in some way, thus leaving Chas as a lodger in her house in her sole charge. She did such odd things, which in my condition, took on a sinister aspect. My sitting-room, at the back of the house on the ground floor, had curtains which didn't quite meet and this witch of a woman would stand outside in the garden and peer through the chinks at me. She once had a strange old man with her and I dashed to the window and held the curtains tight across the gap, my heart pounding, my stomach turning over. One evening I smelt gas and went into the kitchen which was next door to my sitting-room. All the taps on the gas stove were turned on and as I turned them off and opened the window I heard an upstairs door close quietly.

The next day, when Amy was visiting me (she had a council-house near by) and my tormentor was unaware of her presence, she burst into my sitting-room, red and shouting, 'Oh, you stupid woman, you left the gas-taps on last evening, do you want to kill me in my bed?' Then seeing Amy she apologised for being irritable but explained the thought of gas worried her and she would get the gas men in. Perhaps she had been hasty, perhaps there was some fault with the stove. Then she approached me, put her arms round my shoulders and remarked that she was so impatient she couldn't wait until 'our lovely baby' was born. She was sure she would take over from me for she adored babies so. Amy glared at her and remarked to me when the landlady had made her exit, 'Don't let her talk to you like that, Dolly,' but even Amy thought the woman kind at heart and just worried about a gas escape. She added, 'You are a bit absent-minded, Dolly.' At this I burst into tears and Amy, fury subsiding, put her arms round me (she had a bit of a job for I was enormous and she tiny) and said, 'There, there, Dolly, you'll be fine when your baby is here.'

I became mortally afraid to stay alone in the house with my landlady in the winter evenings and as soon as Chas had gone I left too, spending the evenings wandering around the cold dark roads. One winter's night with the snow thick on the ground, I needed a lavatory urgently. I crept on to a building-site, feeling like the naughty cat of my young sister's childhood, and just as I was in the act of crouching, out from the watchman's hut tore an Alsatian dog. I must have been the fastest pregnant harrier ever and gasping for breath arrived back trembling on the front doorstep of 'our' house, aching all over. The key would not unlock the door. The landlady must have put the bolt on yet she knew I was out. I waited in agony for the 'man from the Pru'. He was cross to find me out in such conditions, mine and the weather, but his key turned like magic.

I began to experience such physical irritation as I had never known before, and one day, in desperation, while my landlady was out, I threw myself into a boiling bath, and with a coarse brush and strong carbolic soap I scrubbed and scrubbed and scrubbed. It was sheer heaven—until an hour later when my flesh began to swell and swell and swell and from tummy to knees I was like a skinned balloon. When poor Chas arrived home he almost burst into tears at my inflated state and he helped me so tenderly down the road to see the doctor who lived on the corner. What a sight we were, me so enormous, shuffling with legs a yard apart, poor Chas so slim and worried-looking. The ladies in that road never spoke or even nodded to me, but one lady, peering from behind her stiff starched lace curtains, was so curious as to our strange progress down the road that she actually opened her window and called out, 'Was it an accident?' Game to the last I answered brightly, 'Oh no, we wanted this baby.' Slam went the window. 'Why do you say such things?' said Chas to me gently but reproachfully.

The old doctor rubbed his head when he sighted my self-inflicted injuries and announced that in all his medical experience he'd never come across such a case. He diagnosed baby was blocking something. I'd eaten too many sweets because I had given up smoking and now he wondered if I hadn't chosen the bigger of two evils, the sweets, of course, not the baby. However he was very kind and said I was fortunate to be living with that charming Mrs . . . You too, I thought, yet I *knew* I was right in my fear of the dear woman.

The local insurance office to which Charles was attached was to hold a dinner dance and the new agent *must* attend with his lady and meet the other agents and their wives. I had no decent dress, indeed no dress which would fit, but Chas insisted I go with him and finally I took the sleeves out of a blue winter dress and wore it as a pinafore-dress with a white blouse. I never made up, but I thought that on such an elegant occasion I really should and when I presented myself to Chas (with just a dusting of powder and a *little* lipstick) he was furious and thought I looked like a Jezebel. (Do they get pregnant, I wondered?) So off must come the lipstick, at least. He put my new lipstick down the lavatory and off we went, he slim and elegant in his wedding suit, me large and shiny and, because I'd had my hair cut far too short, looking like an all-in wrestler. (Years later when, a reformed Dorothy, I lived at the home of the Superintendent of the office and his wife because of war-time bombing, he told me he had never forgotten our entrance at the dinner. He thought Chas, a young slim boy, had been trapped by an enormous and elderly woman, although he said it was obvious I was very clever because I won the general knowledge and spelling game they played that night! Chas thought it would have been more diplomatic for me to have lost the game and let someone higher up the strata win. The prize was a make-up kit and ever after Chas never worried whether I made up or not, and I've never learned how to.) No one was brave enough to ask me to dance, although I would not have accepted for fear of shaking my baby about. Chas was very much in demand for he was a very good dancer and the agents' wives all looked so glamorous, beautifully gowned and 'made up'.

I knew we just had to get away from the house in which we were living and I spent the days wandering from estate agent to estate agent. Finally, I passed an agents just opening up in Goodmayes. I was their first customer and they had one house to let. This house, an enormous one, had been converted into two flats and we secured the lower one with an enormous garden. No one ever seemed to look at the top flat and it was like living on an island. There were two huge fireplaces in the lounge, our bedroom had been the library, and my mother lent me the money to purchase sixty yards of curtaining. It was very pretty in pale green and pink stripes, but as I could only spend $4\frac{1}{2}d.$ per yard it was really only the quality of bandage, so that when Chas was away canvassing in the evenings I had to sit in the dark because the lounge was in front of the house and the curtains transparent. The garden was surrounded by a wall which was broken down at the end and whenever I went into the garden to hang out the clothes an enormous German dog would leap over the wall snarling at me. The house had been empty for so long he thought he owned it so Chas had to do what he could to mend the wall, for the dog's owner, also a foreign lady, simply thought it all rather amusing. At first Chas, not being a do-it-yourself man, built the wall, brick symmetrically above brick, so that it all fell down, but he managed it in the end, although we could never sit in the garden and always had one eye on the wall during brief trips, for the German hound was always trying to struggle over.

Our furniture looked like doll's toys in this lovely old house and it was difficult to keep warm unless one crouched over the fire—we couldn't afford two fires. But we were happy there; 'An Englishman's home is his castle', was true for us.

CHAPTER FIVE

Pregnant Pause

With the birth of my first child only weeks away I began to feel very excited, although coupled with the excitement was the fear that because of the previous restless months, fierce dogs, strange landladies and constant upheaval, my baby might have suffered, for Mother had said when hearing of my pregnancy, 'Now, Dolly, relax and think peaceful thoughts, put a beautiful picture above your bed.' She was pleased when she knew everything for baby's needs had been procured, but some people thought it was tempting providence to buy the pram or cot beforehand.

In one way I had been deceitful where the authorities had been concerned but as I deceived them on behalf of my unborn child I stilled my conscience. I had booked in at the maternity wing of Queen Mary's hospital at Stratford when I lived at Forest Gate as it was necessary to make reservations in the very early stages of pregnancy, and it would have been too late to have booked up at a maternity hospital when we moved to Ilford.

We had persuaded my parents to move into the upstairs flat we had left at Forest Gate. This needed all our persuasion for although my mother wanted to move into the same house with Marjorie, my father at first was adamant about leaving dear old Poplar and his friends. Finally when he discovered that at the end of the road was the Clapton football-ground, he fell in with our plans. So I was able, although with such honest parents so respectful of authority I was always a little apprehensive of their acting-a-lie ability, to tutor my mother and father into confirming I was still resident there when the health visitor called to check my residence qualifications for the local hospital.

I tried to dismiss my worries by thinking that my father's 'talking with his hands' act would so mystify any health visitor she might even have felt sorry for me for having such an eccentric parent living with me, and the authorities must have assumed I was still at Forest Gate for the great day came without any prior notification that my bed had been cancelled.

It was only when the great day did arrive, and at the time I was so sure that within a few hours our family would be three in number, that I realised that I should have to journey from Goodmayes to Stratford for the happy event. Chas was late home and I knew I would begrudge him even a few minutes for food. Excitedly I told him my news. Coolly, as though he had been a top gynaecologist all his life, he listened to my 'symptoms', then announced, 'Yes, it is following the correct pattern but I assure you it will be many, many hours yet before things become urgent, as it is your first child.' Then, to my horror he continued, 'I have a death claim to pay, the money is urgently needed, that's why I am late, I have been to the bank. Just rest quietly and I will be back in an hour or so and I promise you we will go immediately.' Off he went on his errand of mercy and 'quietly' I rested all alone, knowing deep down that he was right about my symptoms, but hoping that he wasn't. Dramatically morbid I wanted him to return to find a collapsed wife, a newly born infant, a sort of 'touch and go affair'. The fact that he hadn't stopped one moment for a meal and had nothing to eat or drink all day stemmed not my feelings that he put duty above me.

I sat in my darkening lounge. Men in other houses in that road—one or two even possessed maids—would be home from business and having dinner with their families. I was a stranger to them. How could I burst in in the middle of entrée, soup, or even hors d'oeuvres and announce I was about to give birth? It just wasn't done, that sort of thing. Finally I heard the sound of running feet. A breathless Chas burst in, grabbed my little case which had been packed for weeks and we clambered on to a very shaky 86 bus to Stratford. I was sure I would be accepted as an imminent case; Chas would be remorseful and friends and relations would listen wide-eyed with many 'Oh Dolly's' at my 'casual' tale of near disaster. But the Sister in charge listened aloofly to my urgent story, then to my horror she did a 'Chas' on me and to my husband's great relief she said in the tones of a very kind teacher to a fractious child, 'My dear, *FIRST* babies take *AGES* to be born, you will be unable to get a wink of sleep here. [Sleep!] Go home and have a *LOVELY* night's rest and come and see me in the morning.' I was so desolate that she and Chas had ganged up against me. Sister patted Chas on the back with a look which said, 'Good man.' In my panic and frustration at being sent home I almost blurted out the confidential news that I lived, ineligibly, out of the district. My mother used to say accusingly to me when I was young, 'Good liars, Dolly, need to possess extra good memories,' and I used to feel very injured that of all her children I was singled out for this platitude.

Now that an expert had forecast my child's birth as 'ages' away I felt somewhat guilty at my harsh thoughts about the father of my child. He was the last person to put either of us in danger. He looked pale, and exhausted. In my unthinking panic I had dragged him off without food and he'd been trudging the streets all day. If the boot had been on the other foot I would have been victorious but he tenderly took my hand. As a forgiveness present for him and to ease my guilty feelings I said to the 'no doubt about it Sister', 'That's just what my husband said.' 'Good man, good man,' said a relieved Sister obviously having made up her mind I had been going to insist on 'squatting' in the waiting-room. She and her buddy took me in charge and I was marched off to the exit.

We walked from Stratford to Forest Gate where a worried mother made us a delicious supper, gently chiding Chas, not only because of the shaky bus from Goodmayes (it seemed years ago) but because of our night hike in my condition. She gave us her bed and went off to sleep in my father's room. I heard my father say, with a squeaky giggle 'What's this in aid of, me old gooseberry?' They had had separate rooms for years. She couldn't sleep and neither could I even though my father and Chas were sleeping peacefully. Mother kept putting her head round our bedroom door raising her eyebrows in a sort of query. At last she decided all signs pointed to Queen Mary's and at five a.m. Chas took me to meet the dawn.

I was admitted immediately and handed over to a young probationer nurse for a bath and a shave. The blade was blunt, my young nurse was extremely nervous of the shaving session and to Sister's horror and annoyance I was cut about a bit. 'Oh,' I dismissed my wounds airily, 'It's nothing, Sister, really,' adding, 'I didn't feel a thing.' 'Well,' said Sister, 'I can see we have a model mother here,' then patting my shoulder, she went on with her years of experience of character assessment, 'I knew *you* were going to be no bother.' That same night she must have regretted these words, for without the benefit of anaesthetic I thought the end of the world had come. I had always been told by my teachers and parents that I had a vivid imagination, but what I had imagined was a hundred times more peaceful than the real thing. Doctor was there, in his dressing-gown, with a midwife and a 'learner' nurse. Sister kept dashing into the room from somewhere exhorting me to 'cease my dreadful noise'. At every entry of hers I apologised profusely, it wouldn't happen again I assured her, but no sooner had the door swung on her retreating back than my good intentions were drowned in that valley of torture. 'Take no notice of *her*,' said the doctor (not of course in Sister's presence). 'Just hang on to the cord of my dressing-gown, you're doing fine,' but when I did as he invited he remonstrated, 'Hey, steady on.' Then an elderly doctor brought into the room what appeared to be a large tea-strainer, minus its handle. This was lined with white lint and very gently and kindly he said to me, 'Now as soon as you feel . . .' I guessed the end of the sentence and like a drowning man I buried my head in the tea-strainer and breathed magic ozone. In the quiet and sudden armistice the young doctor said triumphantly, 'Don't you want to see your pretty little daughter,' and I turned my aching neck to see, sitting upright on the midwife's lap, a little crumpled being. The baby, I didn't feel as though she were mine, was very wet-looking. '*This* is the sort of baby *I* like to see,' said the midwife, but I didn't ask what she meant for I was waiting for that FLOOD of mother-love which everyone assured me would permeate my being at the sight of my first born. And I waited, and waited and waited, but nothing came except a feeling of scalding pain. A nurse, giving me tea from a cup with a spout, was so intent on gazing at my baby that she hadn't realised she was sticking the spout down the neck of my gown!

I was then delivered to a ward containing three other 'radiant' mums. I could see why my baby might have been described as 'pretty' for the three occupants, already in residence, of the little swing cots on the ends of the beds, were all boys, all very tiny, all with black coconut thatch hair. They seemed yellowish with rather large mouths, whereas my baby was an 8 lb. girl, with a plump face, a tiny mouth and a little bit of down for hair. Still the surge of mother-love did not come. Instead in came a nurse bearing aloft on a tray three mugs of hot cascara. 'Oh,' she said brightly, 'I didn't know there were four mothers here, I'll fetch another cup,' as though she was bringing sherry to celebrate my arrival. I was unaware that the other mums had been in that ward for nearly a week and were troubled with constipation, and thinking it was all in the day's work, obediently drank the obnoxious fluid.

That evening, the first visiting-time for me, should have been radiant with Chas holding my hand and both of us gazing at our daughter with love and pride. What a time of horror! Mother came with Chas and tutted testily when he announced our daughter was 'Just like his mum.' Now his mum was lovely, but not physically so. Then the cascara decided to make its move. The visiting-time was only half an hour and I had already been regaled by the other mums with the story of the dreadful woman who had previously occupied my bed. She always required attention during visiting hours and no extra time had been granted to the other dads for the time they were turfed out of the ward. So I just would not allow Chas or Mum to find a nurse. They must have loved me very much for between them they raked up five men's handkerchiefs and three paper-bags and by exercising considerable ingenuity I was able to keep going until almost the end of the visiting time. Sister was cross with nurse for giving me the cascara so soon after baby's birth. Nurse stared at me as though I had been stupid to drink it, and my baby cried and cried and cried. In sympathy perhaps. In the end she was taken away from the little flowered cot at the end of my bed and relegated to the linen-cupboard and when I thought of her crying and lonely I too wept into my pillow.

I was looking forward to feeding my daughter. I felt she was crying because she was hungry. I had watched the other mums expertly feed their babies, sliding their large dark brown nipples into their babies' mouths, their breasts huge with milk. Then seen them wind a satisfied and drunken babe. Now I had very tiny nipples which still remained pink, but as my baby had a small mouth I thought nature had matched us up. Until feeding-time that was. It was a superhuman effort to get my baby to open her mouth, then when she did, after a day or two I was bleeding, cracked and sore, and, horror upon horrors, a little piece of nipple was missing. Had she swallowed it? And still she cried and cried and cried. Sister pushed baby's head hard on to me, grumbling when I flinched and in the end Matron said, 'Get your husband to bring you some golden eye ointment.' My father, worried by Mother's tales of a starving child and a maimed and weeping mother, went straight to the chemist for this magic salve and thinking I had the name wrong because the word 'poison' was printed on the tube, decided to wrap it in a note of extra CAUTION. This he intended to leave at the porter's lodge but someone insisted he bring it up to the ward. When he was ushered in it was feeding-time. He was always shy with the opposite sex and I knew he felt his manliness would embarrass the bare-breasted mums. He did a ballet exercise when nurse approached, for he was ever fearful of getting in the way of authority, and nurse was forced to join in this exercise for neither could make up their mind as to which way the other intended to prance. Finally he gave me the package with a hoarse whisper, 'Poison, Dolly, poison, be careful.'

The word 'poison' panicked me as much as it did my father and I waited matron's next morning visit to the ward. She would walk through with an aluminium flour-dredger in her hand, scrape back the clothes on the hanging cots and shake powder all over the babies' umbilical parts. As she left the ward the mothers would crawl down to the ends of the beds, re-arrange the cot clothes and give a glance of hatred towards a receding matron. This morning, trying to appear a competent and unpanicked mother, I said casually to Matron, 'The golden eye ointment is stamped poison, Matron.' She ignored the pathetic plea in my eyes and announced briskly, 'Rub it *well* in, rub it *W-E-L-L* in', just like a military command. But I never used it, terrified I would kill my child.

One day when baby was brought in from the linen-cupboard for her abortive feeding I noticed one of her eyes was closed and inflamed. 'Nurse,' I called. 'Oh,' said nurse, 'that's sticky eye.' Chas, of course, looked this up in the encyclopaedia and discovered it could be a congenital disease. So we had an ancestor somewhere responsible for our baby's trouble. Again a weeping mother, again a cross matron. It wasn't the terrible thing we had thought. The baby had been in a draught and poor nurse was castigated for using this expression. I felt very guilty about this for she was so kind to me.

The other mothers thought us a very strange family, I am sure, for when we were asked for names for our infants, neither Chas nor I had even thought about it. Above my bed was a plaque informing the occupant that the bed had been endowed to the hospital by a Susan Boake, and I thought, 'Well, thank you, Susan, that shall be my daughter's name,' and so she was just Susan. The other mums said it was terrible to give such a pretty baby girl such a plain old-fashioned name when I could have called her 'Pearl', 'Dawn', etc., but I liked the sound of Susan and for once in my life did not change my mind.

When I asked Matron why Susan cried so much she said, 'She is just a bad-tempered baby,' and it seemed that I had so many reasons to weep that I was happy to go home, though not at all confident in my ability to cope. I would sit in my vast bathroom and tremble at baby's bath-time, sure I would let my slippery Susan fall underneath the water and drown. And still she cried. At my first visit to the local clinic the doctor said, 'Why, mother, your baby is completely tongue-tied,' her tongue apparently was fastened, at its tip, to the 'floor' of her mouth by a fine ligament. 'You must call in your own doctor to free the tongue for your baby.' The young local doctor came in that very same evening. Chas boiled his equipment. I held Susan, and Chas held my hand while the doctor performed this minor, but frightening to us, operation. 'Susan,' laughed the doctor. 'You gave her the right name for a tongue-tied baby, Thoothan.' After the deed was done he said, 'Put her to the breast for comfort, Mother.' Then he gazed intently at my bosom, gave it an extremely hard squeeze and announced, 'Good God, woman, you have no milk,' adding to Chas, 'Dash down to the chemist and get some dried milk.' Chas chose Cow and Gate and from that moment on Susan became the loveliest, happiest and sweetest baby I think it was possible to have. I felt so guilty about the early weeks of her life spent half-starving in a linen-cupboard, that I made up my mind to try and think for myself in future.

At Susan's christening when she was in the tongue-tied, half-starved state she had cried all the time and at the party afterwards, when both Chas's family and mine were present, I had forbidden anyone to pick her up for I had been informed by 'authority' that babies should only be nursed at feeding-time. I recall the two grannies nearly in tears at what they thought was my harsh attitude and lack of maternal feeling for they gave me severe looks every time I passed them. But neither of them was brave enough to argue with me. I could cry myself now when I remember I wouldn't allow those two dear grannies to pick up and nurse their little grand-daughter.

And as for that feeling of flooding mother-love. I believe it does not come flooding at all, I believe it comes as the seconds, minutes and hours go by caring for a helpless creature.

Our vast rooms needed more human habitation than Chas, baby and I could supply and we were happy to have our parents stay some week-ends. Chas's parents visited first. Now Chas should have been the chef of the family, possibly because he loved cooking, he was the expert, well, more the expert than I was. He had some bee in his bonnet, possibly associated with an early childhood memory, that his father was fond of, even crazy about, oxtail. This puzzled me for I had been to lunch with my in-laws on many many Sundays and it was always the usual roast and I knew if Alfred, my father-in-law, was so crazy about oxtail, Ethel, his wife, would have been happy to prepare it for him.

But Chas insisted oxtail took over a day to prepare, that was why his busy mother prepared it so infrequently. He would take care of the oxtail main course, I would be the sweet chef. I was happy about this for I had no more desire to cook than I had to spit and polish. I could therefore make various fruit pies and banish myself from the kitchen leaving the 'galley' to him. He cooked the oxtail twice so that every vestige of fat could be removed, for oxtail is a very fatty meat. He took hours grating finely the various assorted vegetables.

The great day came and Ethel, Alfred and Dolly were seated expectantly at the table, snowy white cloth, shining glass. Alfred was hungry and excited, it was such a cold day. Chas entered with our beautiful china serving-bowl, a wedding present, and with all the professional know-how of his waiting years, served us all with his lovingly prepared oxtail. After the hours and hours of cooking I thought it looked only like thick soup, and I thought also that Alfred, like a little boy, looked as though he would burst into tears for I was sure he had been looking forward to roast sirloin.

As Chas left with the dirty dishes, Alfred said in a stage whisper to Ethel, 'What a disappointing meal, whatever was it? I was so sure we'd have a real meal, especially on a Sunday!' 'Hush, man,' said Ethel sharply. 'That girl has done her best, she has a young baby to look after, you know.' But he was full of praise for my redcurrant and raspberry tart with thick cream. Chas told his mother *he* had chosen and prepared the oxtail thinking to delight his father and she said, 'Lor luv you, bor, years ago he would have been, it's not stews on Sundays now.' Not only had Alfred a regular job as a storekeeper, now that all his children were married, he was able to let the upstairs flat in his house thus receiving a weekly rent. If his upstairs tenant had a baby or children, then he was doubly delighted.

The following week-end it was the turn of my parents, who came with Marjorie, now pregnant, and her Alfred. Chas, quite disinterested in the Sunday lunch this time, left all culinary arrangements to me and took charge of Susan. At the first peal of the doorbell I rushed to let my folks in, hardly recognising Marjorie. Someone, possibly Mother, had advised her, that because of her condition, warm, sensible clothes should be worn. She had been in her interesting condition for a few weeks only, yet there she stood like a refugee from Lapland, clad in Mother's famous kangaroo coat that my sister Winifred had sent her from Australia. Grey woollen stockings, flat heeled ward-maid's shoes and a matronly 'toque' completed her outfit. Much to Mother's indignation I became hysterical, although my unrestrained laughter finally infected her as well as for the first time she really 'sighted' Marjorie. Marjorie could see no humour in the situation and was politely aloof, at the same time a little hurt. Dolly was now a fully fledged mother, and having experienced this expectant condition such a short time ago, surely a sisterly, sympathetic squeeze of the hand was not too much to expect. I was sorry I had laughed at Marjorie's maternity outfit and was almost calm and compassionate to the 'little' mother-to-be, when my father, who had been sitting on a hall chair slowly rose, saying in broken English, 'You give my bear bread my bear he dance for you.' He then pivoted slowly around singing in a grunting tone, 'Ronnie ronnie ron ronnie ron ron ron.' His impromptu mime of the dancing bears of his childhood was so expertly executed, so delightfully comical, his face so dazedly yet wickedly bear-like, I had to dash off to the kitchen to restrain a further bout of laughter. The dance finished I heard my father's high pitched giggle and Mother's reproving, 'What *has* got into you, Walter, you've always said how nice I always looked in that coat.' Obviously through the years my father *had* thought the coat a comical affair but if it had pleased Mother it really hadn't worried him what she wore, as long as she was decently covered.

My folks were to spend the night with us and all went well until the next morning. After an Arctic night all the pipes became frozen. Father attended to these, so eager to put the sanitation right for us that he worked on them in his best Sunday suit. He thoroughly enjoyed his week-end much to his surprise. He had not wanted to visit us, preferring to stay at home, home being the only place in which he really felt relaxed. His home-made barrel arm-chair, his library-books, his pipe, he preferred these simple things. He did not need people or social occasions, but he was happy at my house for that week-end for he felt he had been useful to us. The icy weather, however, vindicated Marjorie's furry covering.

Apart from our parents we did not receive many visits from the rest of the family. They were scattered far and wide across the country and fares had to be reckoned with for few people had cars. Agnes and Amy, however, lived within a few minutes' walk of our house and I saw them often.

Agnes was going through a rough period for her husband, Arthur, had lost his job in the City because of the depression and as he was over fifty—and unemployment was still a problem in the thirties—he'd had successive casual work, odd jobs for odd days, until finally he obtained a job as a baker's roundsman. He was not really strong enough to be a human horse, the bakers' vans in those days had shafts, but he was pleased to take any job, and this one he tackled with great courage. Soaked to the skin on cold wet winter days he still had a cheery word and smile for his customers and was very popular with them. I passed him while shopping one day, when a woman called out from an upstairs window, it was absolutely teeming with rain. He had already called at this house and she said, 'I forgot to ask you, baker, have you a small brown one?' His cheerful reply was so naughty but so comical the customer was in hysterics. Here was a man, well read, a wizard with figures, a cultured man, yet he was making the best of things in those depressing days, and he was only one of many men forced to live like that. Agnes always had a ready smile for me and never moaned about her luck. She used to take pupils for shorthand but they were neighbours' children and she only charged one shilling for one evening's tuition.

Before his permanency as a baker's roundsman the Labour Exchange had provided Arthur with an odd week's work, here and there. At one time he was employed on the incinerator at a local hospital, and then Amy's Jimmy managed to get him a job on a ship which had been in the Docks for some time and it looked as though this ship would be static for many months more. Arthur was a sort of odd job 'boy' among the skeleton caretaker crew. However, after only two weeks on this ship, suddenly sailing orders were received. Arthur was offered a permanent job at £1 13*s.* 4*d.* a month, impossible of course, with a wife and three little children.

The ship was sailing from Tilbury and on the afternoon of the sailing the Bosun asked Arthur if he would be kind enough to take his pet dog home to his wife in North London. Quite a journey, but the wife, the Bosun assured Arthur, would be overjoyed to receive her husband's most treasured possession. It was a dreadful journey in pouring rain, buses and trains, and long waits in between. On one bus the poor animal was sick and Arthur was turned off the bus. The thought of a nice meal and warm welcome from the Bosun's wife, kept him going and finally he arrived at the house in North London. The door opened at his ring and a large bad-tempered looking woman appeared. Arthur, wet, cold and tired (he had another rotten journey from there to his home at Dagenham, to face yet) waited for the woman to recognise her husband's dog, but after Arthur finished his tale of the Bosun's love-token the woman screamed, 'You can take the bloody dog off, I'm not looking after that bloody thing for that miserable bugger.' She slammed the door shut, and Arthur realised, through the Bosun's wife's choice of definitive words, that there was no point in ringing again. He wandered round the North London roads. What could he do about the dog? He couldn't take it home, Agnes and the children were barely existing, they couldn't manage to feed a dog. If he took it to the Police Station there would be forms to fill in and perhaps they wouldn't take the dog. He found himself back at the railway station. The lost property and cloakroom was open. He gazed through the steamy windows and saw a blazing coke fire. Sitting by the fire was a porter, a jolly looking man, and at the counter was an elderly clerk. These men were both laughing at some joke they were having. Arthur was drawn like a magnet to this human warmth and he entered with his hound. The counter was high and as he stood there, the dog went round the counter to the fire and lay down in front of it. 'Oh, you poor old dear,' said the jolly porter. 'And where did you come from? Why you're all wet.' 'Is he yours?' asked the clerk of Arthur. 'No,' said Arthur, to his eternal shame. 'He must have run in when I opened the door,' praying that the dog would not turn round, recognise him and come back. 'Poor thing!' said the clerk. 'Give him a rub down, Joe,' he said to the porter, 'and I'll find something for him to eat.' Arthur asked a simple enquiry of the clerk, and left the station quickly. He often wondered what happened to the dog, easing his conscience that at least he had left the poor unwanted animal in kindly hands.

He arrived home in the dark, to find Agnes and the three children asleep on makeshift beds in the sitting-room. They all had 'flu and thinking Arthur was still employed on the boat

Agnes had brought the children down into the room with a fire. 'I thought you were at Tilbury,' she said. 'Oh, no,' said Arthur, 'I've been to see a Bosun's wife about a dog.' Agnes thought he too, was starting 'flu.

Things were more comfortable for Amy because her James had a good regular job. They were buying a new house and Amy had furnished this tastefully with cushions, curtains and furnishings beautifully embroidered by her. Amy was *born* a liberated woman. She used to take my breath away at her instant reactions. I just loved to spend the day with her and sit by at bath-time when her son was a baby. She was bathing him one evening, preparatory to his evening meal. He was a large, strong, healthy babe, he seemed to make Amy look so tiny. He was yelling for his feed and Amy was valiantly trying to bath him properly although his struggles were strong for a baby. As his crying got more frantic, Jim, who had been pacing up and down worried that his son was crying, suddenly stopped his pacing, and said to Amy, 'Are you sure, Cheggie dear, you are not getting soap into his eyes?' Up jumped a flushed and furious Amy, smack went a wet soapy flannel across Jim's face. 'He hasn't any soap in his eyes but I'm sure you have soap in yours now.' Jim left the room. Amy having finished the bath torture, was feeding a quiet happy babe at her breast. On her face was a look of ecstasy.

We got on so well together at this stage (not being under the same roof) that I often wondered if she regretted not taking me out when I was a little girl. Although I had been a plain thin child, as tall as Amy at 13, and Marjorie her constant companion was small with flaxen curls and large brown eyes, I would have made a better decoy duck for Amy, for that was what Marjorie really was, although she may not have known it. I would have been of more use, for although more naïve than the other girls, I did possess a certain guile, a shrewdness for summing up situations, which Marjorie never did—always artless and open, always scrupulously honest. I would have known the opportune moment for Amy to turn round on her promenade along the main road so that she would 'accidentally' bump into the man (or men) of her choice, whereas Marjorie had to be continually questioned by Amy—'Are they turning round, are they looking back?' One day one of Amy's admirers was pacing up and down the Grove, not yet on the important enough guest list for him to be able to call at the house. Marjorie went out to play, naturally this young man knew she was 'Amy's sweet little baby sister'! 'Is Amy coming, is she ready?' asked this so eager young man (all Amy's young men were so eager for her company). 'Oh, no,' replied honest Marjorie. 'She's still fast asleep in bed!' We did, on rare occasions, get a little benefit from Amy's male associations, for one young man, bidding her a sad adieu when he was going to the seaside with his family was asked by Amy to 'bring her back a stick of rock'. She was only joking but an enormous parcel arrived, the young man had ordered a special stick to be made. It was so enormous the postman could hardly carry it!

Amy's James thought us a callous family on the whole. If I was ill in bed, Mother would do her best to spare me all the time she could out of her busy life, but no one visited from the rest of the family, they just rushed up with a meal for the invalid, bashed it down on a chair by the bed and were off immediately to their more worthwhile pursuits. James said one day, 'I can't understand it, if my brother or sisters were in bed sick, why the rest of us would take it in turns to sit with the invalid, and we would save our pocket money, if only to be able to take a bag of acid-drops to him.' Now Jimmy was not yet married to Amy, therefore he was not a 'fully paid-up member' of the clan. It was all right for us to criticise the family, indeed we did it all the time (it was one of our favourite pastimes!), but at criticism of each other from an outside source, we immediately 'closed ranks'. 'Well,' said Amy tartly (probably knowing Jim was right, but he came of a gentle, close family), 'Acid-drops are a perfect invalid diet, of course.'

I was surprised, one day, to see Amy's friend, Helen, shopping alone. Amy, apparently, was in bed, very poorly with a sore throat. I arranged to call at Amy's house early the next morning and Helen said she would let Amy know. I let myself in the back door of Amy's house the following day and called, 'Cooee, Amy, it's Dolly,' as I went up the stairs. The bedroom door was flung open and a sobbing hysterical Amy appeared. 'I told her she wasn't my sister, you are my sister, Dolly,' she wept. Tucked up in bed she tried to tell me what had upset her. She felt so ill she was longing for me to arrive when the door-bell sounded. She was sure it was me and had gone down the stairs to open the door and say, 'Oh, Dolly, thank you for coming,' but no sister Dolly smiling there. Instead, according to Amy, there stood an enormous woman. Amy, apparently had burst into tears and cried, 'Oh, I thought you were my sister,' and this large female personage had cried dramatically, 'I *am* your sister, I have come to bring you to Jesus.' Amy, terrified (probably not ready for such a journey), had slammed the door. I calmed Amy down and assumed she was delirious, for when the doctor called he pronounced that she had 'quinsy'. The next day, however, I was at home expecting Agnes to call. The bell rang and I tore to the door. No Agnes, but a very large female. 'I was expecting my sister,' I said, looking down the road to see if Agnes was coming. 'I *am* your sister,' commenced the large lady. 'Ho, ho,' I thought, this must be Amy's caller, possibly an only child gone peculiar with longing for a sister. 'You should be more careful going round the roads frightening people,' I said to her. 'Who could be frightened of the Lord?' she said dramatically. 'God is *Love*.' At last the penny dropped; of course, she was a Jehovah's Witness. Feeling sorry that I had accused her of being a frightener I asked her in for a cup of tea. Agnes arrived and I left the two 'sisters' together chatting amicably. At that time Agnes was interested in spiritualism, so if the J.W. hadn't obtained two converts, at least she had had an interesting half-hour.

I went to the spiritualist church one Sunday with Agnes, but it didn't do anything for me. I presumed I was too worldly, but one girl told me her spiritual guide, an Asian named Golden Feather, had helped her financially. This girl's husband was a spendthrift and Golden Feather, so the girl assured me, had advised her from his spiritual plane, to charge her husband money each time he wished to make love to her. In this way, being of a loving nature, he would not be able to be so much of a spendthrift, at least not when absent from home. She said it worked very well in the beginning but one night her husband was 'broke' and in a weak moment, having such a large 'kitty' she lent him the money, thus causing the system to break down, for she told me, 'Now he is always on the borrow.' She looked at me vacantly when I said, 'And what does Golden Feather say now?'

I was always restless, anxious for things to change, never contented with 'sufficient unto the day', I decided the flat upstairs (no one ever came to view it) was more attractive than the one downstairs, and without consulting Chas I asked the agent, who called weekly for the rent, if we could change over. He was a small, polite man, for ever announcing proudly to me that 'he possessed a pigeon pair'. At that time I had no idea what he was talking about, and was surprised some years later to learn that a pigeon pair is a son and daughter.

The agent gave his consent and Chas arrived home one day to find us safely installed upstairs. Although he agreed it looked cosier he was furious I hadn't forewarned him. He said his heart leapt at the sight of the downstairs curtainless windows. He thought Susan and I had been mysteriously abducted. (With our furniture?) He hadn't glanced at the upstairs windows. He looked so shaken he had to sit down.

I assured my darling that now I was content and he really believed me (perhaps my mother might have warned him). One morning he was to attend an important meeting at his company's divisional offices. Susan was awake at dawn and I fed her in the kitchen, loth to wake Chas, always wanting people to forget their worries in blessed sleep. With Susan asleep in her pram in the kitchen I crept back to the bedroom for my clothes. Sudden inspiration came to me as I gazed round the bedroom. It would look much better as a sitting-room. On to the floor I emptied the contents of my immense bevelled wardrobe. Excitedly I dragged the wardobe, after me, to the door. It was almost on to the landing when the door sprang open. The wretched bevelled door had jammed the wardrobe between bedroom and stair banisters, trapping me on the kitchen side of the flat, and worse still, Chas in the bedroom. The noise of my struggles finally woke him. 'What the hell is going on?' he shouted. 'It's all right,' I said, trying to be calm. 'Just pull the wardrobe your way, its not heavy, I've emptied it.' It was impossible to move it. Chas, the time getting on, was frantic, not only about his attendance at the important meeting, but his morning visit to the bathroom was becoming increasingly urgent.

In the end an irate, unshaven, unrelieved husband left the house by tying two sheets together, making a fireman's exit. I thought he was very callous to leave me trapped in my night-dress. It took me two hours to work the banister-rail loose and my shiny bevelled wardrobe was permanently indented. Chas had to spend precious money for a shave at the barber's and wondered if his long delay in visiting a lavatory had not caused permanent damage. 'When things are going all right, why the hell can't you let well alone?' he asked on his return. I was meekly submissive for a few days.

CHAPTER SIX

Evacuees

Susan was about six weeks old when war was declared. As the solemn announcement ended I looked out of the window. The siren went, making an awful noise, and a man ran along the road wearing a gas-mask. Each time he reached a kerb he lifted up his gas-mask to negotiate it. Chas and I had indulged in cross words when collecting baby's immense mask. He wanted a practice go with her in it but I thought the contraption looked so terrible it might suffocate her when there might never even be a gas raid.

Jimmy, Amy's husband, was very worried about Amy and her son and daughter being near London now that the war had started so with her children and my babe we travelled down to Wales to Winifred's in-laws, where, because I had spent happy childhood hours, I imagined all would be the same. Of course disillusion was in store for us. The parents were dead, and the youngest son had married. They welcomed us in their own way but were very busy, having made the inn, in which they lived, very popular. It was full to capacity in the evenings with army and air force personnel and salesmen, and amongst the salesmen was a young man who seemed to have a penchant for Amy's young son, by now a boy of twelve, a good-looking and extremely charming lad. This worried us both; we had no man to turn to for advice. Food was sparse, but Susan was all right for we had purchased enough baby food to last her for a whole year. Amy worked hard there for mine host would purchase furniture at auctions as the inn had many bedrooms, and Amy would scrub and polish this second-hand furniture for him. Then she would help get the bedrooms ready for more residents. John, our host, belonged to the local volunteer force and one night Amy was woken up by the sound of stones being thrown against her bedroom window. John was needed for an emergency which had arisen in an outlying village. His bedroom was at the back of the inn down a maze of narrow corridors, all pitch dark because heavy curtains had been fixed up because of the blackout and there was no lighting above stairs in the inn. She found his bedroom by the light of matches but on the way back, having used her last match, lost her way in the terrible blackness. She was afraid to call out in case she woke the children and frightened them and stayed lost in the utter darkness until dawn.

Hungry and more worried and miserable each day Amy said to me, 'Oh, Dolly, you are the one with ideas, can't you think of a solution for us now?' This rare compliment from a member of my family I accepted as a real challenge and visited shops and houses enquiring for rooms to let. I discovered that up in the hills was a small farm where they might be prepared to let rooms. We hadn't cottoned on to the propaganda that 'careless talk costs lives' and 'don't talk to a stranger' and when we got outside the village we found all the signposts had been removed. We asked a group of children which way to go. They just stared and then decided to follow us. We went up the mountain like the Pied Piper, for children seemed to come from nowhere to join our first 'admirers'. We came to the gates of a large mansion and decided to enter and ask directions there. This caused much giggling amongst the crowd of children and I wondered who the large house belonged to. The owners were away and a rosy cheeked parlour-maid must have seen nothing sinister in us, or like us hadn't heard about fifth columns, for she gave us directions immediately adding, 'It's very lonely up there.' The ascent to the farm was so steep we all clung on to Susan's pram and I was pleased when we reached the farm where the farmer's wife, who could talk only Welsh-English, showed us the rooms she was prepared to let to us. They were quite nice but my mind and eyes were on the strange animal tied up outside the farm. I supposed it was a dog but it wasn't like any dog I had seen before. Its fur was a sort of dark mauvy brown, its face was heart shaped, it was extremely low to the ground and running down its back was a dirty white stripe. Seeing the puzzlement on my face the farmer's wife said, 'I've chained him up today as he is a bit sassy with childer, it's the nineener in him.' We arranged to take the rooms but half way down the steep and dangerous incline, it hit me like a bomb. 'Nineener' was, of course, 'hyena'. So the dog was part hyena; and the 'sassy' meant he'd have the baby. We all knew we couldn't take the rooms then. Well, they *were* isolated.

In desperation I went to the local Town Clerk, a charming man. He understood our problems perfectly, fell in love with the baby and the other two children and took us straight across the road to a lovely house to visit his mother. She too was enamoured of the baby and offered us a suite of rooms. There was no rent, or heat or light to pay for, the billeting allowance would be sufficient. All we need do was to feed ourselves. Until rationing proper came in and we were issued with ration-books, although things were not yet short, we had great difficulty in obtaining certain commodities in the village, and the next town was about seventeen miles away! We were the first people there so early on in the war and we stuck out like a sore thumb as 'foreigners'. It mattered not that we had a sister who had married a local boy. We were Londoners. It mattered not that we bought all our other goods there, sugar, flour, tea and coffee was denied to us. Naturally the shopkeepers felt they should keep any stocks, which might became scarce, for their own people. So of course we had to get parcels 'from home'.

The village doctor was quite a character, very ancient and a 'teat-hater'. He would roam the village like a vampire, almost dressed for the part, and carrying a long unrolled umbrella would search 'his' babies' prams. With the long pointed end of his umbrella crammed with 'dummies', he would return gleefully to his surgery and cast them on to his fiery furnace. At his approach mothers could always be seen 'tidying' prams so that it seemed babies would suddenly yell when the doctor was only just 'sighted'.

So followed some very happy months, apart from the fact that we were away from our menfolk. Susan was an ideal baby, Rodney, Amy's son, went to the local grammar school and made a good friend. Angela was unhappy at starting a new school with children who spoke differently from her and I felt very sorry for her, but gradually she appeared to settle down. After the noisy inn it seemed like paradise and our hostess even put her store of preserved fruits and jams at our disposal. She was a small aristocratic looking old lady, and had obviously been used to commanding people all her life. She possessed a 'daily', a young strong healthy girl who attended from early morning until late evening, cycling in from one of the outlying villages. This girl's first duty was to light the old-fashioned kitchen-range-stove in the enormous stone-floored kitchen. Our hostess called the girl 'the domestic' and Amy, like my father always on the side of the under-dog, was upset at the mundane life the girl led. She seemed to imagine that the girl, who lived with her grandparents, might have been born illegitimately and felt that the old lady used the girl and was in some way punishing her for the circumstances of her birth. But *if* this was so, I either ignored it, or stilled my conscience, for the old lady couldn't have been kinder or gentler to Susan and the older children. The house was lovely and I couldn't see much sense, from my selfish point of view, in being a crusader at such a time and educating 'the domestic' to discover that there was a brighter and easier life somewhere else. She had been content and happy before we arrived and I hardly felt it was up to us to sow in her the seeds of revolt.

The gardener had been 'called to the colours' and so we decided, by taking over the care of the large garden, that we would be repaying in some measure our hostess's kindness to us. She was absolutely delighted and told us to throw the grass cuttings over the hedge into the field which backed on to our garden. We worked hard and happily all day and as we tossed the last of the garden rubbish over the tall hedge, over the top of it climbed a large black creature—the local coal merchant. He was screaming and shouting at the top of his voice, 'Bloody hoo, bloody hoo, there's hoo in it, hoo in it.' Out marched the old lady and in a voice of command ordered the coal merchant to be off, but he was in a fearful rage and when we understood why we felt very sorry for him. He had no need of subservience to the old lady. He owned his own business and apparently there was a feud between them, for in the old lady's garden rubbish were yew-tree clippings and of course yew was poison to his horses which grazed in the field where the lady disposed of garden refuse. We climbed into the field and cleared it of any danger to the horses and he calmed down, pacified to know that while we were in residence his horses would be safe.

My elder sister Winifred was in Australia. At the age of 40 she became pregnant for the first time after longing for a baby all her married life. This meant they would both have to leave their jobs as it was a joint appointment. War had broken out and they decided to come home and live in Wales with Syd's people. They had a tortuous journey, having to take to the boats and it was feared Winnie's baby would be born at sea, but she arrived in Wales a week or so before her daughter was born. She must have felt very frightened in an open boat with lurking German submarines. Certainly there were better places (and a better audience) one could wish for as a maternity unit, although the 'Lots and lots of water' requested by those in charge on such occasions, would have been fulfilled. We were excited for her because of the baby and thrilled to think she would be living in a cottage in the village. It seemed as though we were building up a little Cheggie community in Wales, even though the three of us now possessed different surnames.

Winifred hurried to visit us after her arrival and we listened avidly to her experiences in the Australian bush. The loss of all her possessions in a bush fire, the hard slog to start their wheat farm, the near misses with poisonous snakes, the shooting of dingoes for which she received one shilling per head from the Australian authorities. We didn't like the part where she shot the pretty little pink and grey birds making a long string of the heads for which she also received payment because they were a pest to the crops. It seemed hardly possible this was Winifred the ex-bank clerk with the dainty hands. The life she had led was tough and raw and I knew that within me was no pioneer for I would have returned on the next boat. Winnie the fearless I thought her.

She had literally taken the doctor's advice to put her feet up as much as possible and had taken her shoes off and was resting them on a dining-room chair as a footstool when the old lady came in to say 'hallo' to the wanderer. Winnie was charming but spoke to the old lady as though she was an equal. Had it been me I would have jumped up in a more respectful stance but Winnie and Amy just laughed at my humility.

Amy received money regularly from her husband but it was a struggle for Chas to send me much, having to keep two homes going in a manner of speaking, as he hadn't been at his job for long, so that when the old lady's son, having become Food Officer, asked me if I would like to open the Food Office proper I jumped at the idea. My wages would be 25*s.* per week. An empty building in the village was put at my disposal, a carpenter was provided to make what shelves and cupboards I needed and Amy said she would take care of Susan. I worked from nine a.m. to five p.m. from then on. Forms of all numbers, sizes and colours arrived and I worked so conscientiously that soon all was ship-shape and Bristol fashion, and I could find in a split second any form required. We took in the outlying districts and as there was an influx of people because of the war, it was decided as I was overworked that a young local girl should be employed to 'assist' me. My assistant had never worked in an office before but she felt, although she never said it in so many words, that as she was a 'national' and me a 'furiner' the town was hers by birthright, and very soon the whole office routine was altered. Ever after it was difficult to find an appropriate form and people were forced to wait ages for attention, but I wondered if she was not brighter psychologically than I was, because we appeared to be so busy dashing about from cupboard to cupboard and room to room searching for a certain form or regulation it was said, 'Those two gels are doing a grand job for the war, look you.'

Amy missed her husband so much (and he missed her even more) that she was persuaded to go up to London for the week-end where she had a happy time. We had a fine time in Wales too for we paddled in the little Welsh streams and picnicked in the beautiful countryside and the people were so welcoming and warm. We pretended there was no war, that we were on an extended holiday. When I had put the children to bed the old lady invited me to take supper with her and we supped and dined on beautiful china, silver and linen, afterwards going through her marvellous family albums. Children on ponies, men in wigs and gowns or officers' uniforms, children with nannies, young people in Switzerland. It really was another world, yet in spite of everything, I felt the old lady was just a granny at heart and she really did treat me as a respected guest. Too, I felt her loneliness and I knew why she loved our children.

However, the rot began to set in, the 'domestic' really did wonder 'how green is my valley' and decide things were brighter beyond it. With the 'domestic' gone the old lady fell ill. Amy took charge and became a hard-working and compassionate nurse to her, but because of Amy's willingness the old lady perhaps began to see her as a replacement for the girl and began to ring for Amy each morning with a, 'Now for my breakfast this morning I will have a little . . .' This early morning confrontation was a comical sight, although I couldn't expect either Amy or the old lady to find any humour in it. The old lady wore fabulous boudoir caps of satin, laced and be-ribboned, but by dawn the cap was always askew and the two little lace ear-pieces were not in their proper place, but one on the forehead and one on the back of her head. She could not have observed Amy's demeanour whilst she 'chose' her menu for I thought Amy looked as though she should be wearing the pointed striped tricolour cap of the French revolution, listening for tumbril-wheels and shouting, 'To the Bastille.'

Of course I was at work and there was the difficult task first thing in the morning of igniting the kitchen monster before even a kettle could be boiled. Of all the family Amy had the most modern home, yet she didn't mind the hard work and inconvenience. It was the old lady's commanding manner which finally wore down Amy's patience and caused her fiery nature to erupt.

The old lady had one fidgety habit. Her front doorstep must always be pristinely pure in its snowy whiteness, never must a human footfall despoil its virgin appearance, and rather than tempt providence we had, all of us, always used the back entrance down a long stone passage, through the wood-cellar and into the kitchen. When we emerged out of this darkness into light I would notice that the pupils on Susan's eyes were enormous. However, one morning when Amy was rushed off her feet, the stove bad tempered and smoky, the children dashing about to be in time for school, me getting ready for work, there came a haughty muttering from the old lady in the hall. 'Someone' had trodden on the freshly cleaned doorstep. The old lady's continued ill-timed complaints were the tinder sparks which lit the furious fire which followed. A noisy argument broke out between her and Amy which, continuing into the lounge, became a fierce and frightening row. I listened at the door. How could I go in and try to pour oil on troubled water? Amy would naturally expect me to be on her side and I could understand this. But the old lady was 'eightyish'; how could two younger women be against her? It was *her* house, *her* step which had been despoiled, and she had been exceptionally kind to the children. I didn't know which way to turn and when I heard the old lady say to Amy, 'You are so different from your sister. I could have lived with her peaceably,' I knew this would be the final straw and I went upstairs to pack. Amy came upstairs, still flushed and said to me, 'You are a hypocrite, Dolly. The old lady says if we are not out by the morning she will call the police.'

Five refugees left, at dawn, the following day. It was cold with a biting Welsh mist. I had been so modern in my care of Susan she had never worn a bonnet and I vaguely remember worrying because her forehead had a sort of mauve tinge.

Amy and I were silent until we had to change trains. There had been some trouble on the line and the platform was crowded with women, children, prams and babies. Standing near us was a lady, clad in furs, and carrying a small dog. They seemed, both of them, to be sniffing in a superior manner. It was obvious she would not get a seat for herself and her companion on the next train due in and she said in a haughty manner, 'Just look at them all, it's typical of the lower classes, they run at the first sign of danger.' 'Yes,' I agreed. 'To you we may be the great unwashed, but if the working man, our husbands and sons, were not so bravely fighting Hitler, you wouldn't be standing on an English station worrying about getting a seat for that sniffing creature.' Poor little doggie, he'd done no one any harm, he wasn't even responsible for his haughty mistress. But my outburst pleased Amy mightily and she half forgave me my cowardice in Wales.

My eldest sister Agnes was with Chas to meet us at Paddington. They looked pale and tired but were delighted to see us again. Agnes took Susan on her lap and was so intent on listening to Amy's excited news that she really wasn't concentrating on holding baby and Susan had somehow fallen forward in the crook of Agnes's arm and looked helpless and dribbling. Chas inspected her worriedly and enquired, 'Is she all right mentally?' This infuriated Amy and she said to Chas, 'Well, that's a kind remark to greet your wife with.' I knew then that she and I were friends again, but I understood my husband. Had there been anything wrong with his daughter that I hadn't discovered, he wanted to bring it to my notice so that anything amiss might be put right with the appropriate and speedy treatment. He really does possess the critical eye. He couldn't know then that he had nothing to fear in that direction. Susan was to become exceptionally bright and top of the school.

CHAPTER SEVEN

The Woman from the Pru

At home, what a sight met my eyes. The house smelt musty and damp, and seemed to be filled to capacity with strange bits of shabby furniture. Chas, unable to stand the loneliness of the large house without Susan and me, had gone to live with my eldest sister Agnes who had a house near by, and sure I was away for the duration of the war, had allowed people to store their bits and pieces, free of charge, in our large rooms, the men being in the forces and the women and children evacuated. In this way they were able to relinquish their houses without worrying about their furniture for they would have been unable to pay rent on the houses whilst their men were away and they had to support themselves and their children in the country. To add to the dismal appearance of the house the curtains were hanging in tatters. Chas, always careless I felt where lighted matches were concerned, had blown a match 'out' and dropped it into the waste-paper-basket, and the curtains being cheap muslin were alight in a matter of seconds.

Then the blow fell. Although we had paid our rent regularly the agents had not paid the rates which were included in our rent and we were summoned by the council. I thought they'd have plenty to distrain upon in our house, but I realised we couldn't go on living as we were. The council were very helpful regarding all our problems and offered us a council-house at Dagenham as so many people were dashing off into the country to avoid the raids.

The new residence had a very large garden which had been badly neglected. Chas decided he'd still have time to dig for victory before he was called up and attacked the forest of weeds the very day we moved in. As the furniture-van departed came a knocking at the door, and as I opened it a sallow-faced dark-haired woman marched straight into the house. She went from room to room downstairs and I followed her helplessly. Suddenly she said, in a tone of incredulity, 'Ain't you got no pianner?' 'No,' I stammered apologetically. 'Ain't you even got a china cabinet?' 'No,' I said. 'Oh,' she said, in tones of utter disbelief, 'I said to my husband, by the looks of her, they'll be bound to have a piano and a china cupboard.' I felt quite ashamed to have let this neighbour down, and I couldn't think how my appearance could have deceived her into thinking I was musical, and as for the china cabinet, there was definitely nothing porcelain about me.

Chas's garden positively flourished and the man next door (husband of the disappointed lady) was disgusted. He would gaze at his garden, which, according to him, he worked at ceaselessly but which looked like the Sahara with a bit of green showing here and there. He would complain of his bad luck and be quite insulting about Chas's 'good luck', but finally he achieved a small success with some broad beans. Now, as every gardener knows, broad beans are a magnet for black fly and his were literally crawling with the creatures. We were in the garden one day when he called to us, 'You see what luck I have, no one else gets black fly but me.' Chas was about to tell him what to do towards a cure (and why he had black fly), when I stopped him for I knew the man would not take any advice kindly. 'I know what I'll do,' he said victoriously. 'I'll do something to kill the buggers once and for all, they'll never come in my garden again.' Chas was very interested, always eager for any new tips about vegetable growing and pest control. As the man re-emerged from his house carrying two kettles of bubbling, boiling water, I knew what he planned to do. I fled into the house, but Chas, either disbelieving, or transfixed, I don't know which, stayed, watching the approaching Jonah as though paralysed. The man went from plant to plant pouring boiling water on to them. As he reached the last plant he turned round triumphantly to view the millions of dead black insects, but the beans were already doing their dying swan act and the man jumped up and down in his garden in fearful rage. He knew I was watching for I couldn't get back from the window quickly enough and he shouted, 'You don't get my bloody luck, do you? It's not fair, it's not fair,' and away he went indoors where we could hear a fearful row going on between him and his wife. She was sure we were to blame. After all, what can you say about people who look as though they possess a 'pianner' and don't?

But I know how easy it is to put failures down to 'bad luck' for I thought I had sheer bad luck when cooking. Chas was for ever on about his mother's steak and kidney puddings. Although I was scared of ever trying to make one, I thought perhaps as he was soon to leave us that if I tried my best, he would remember his wife's delicious pudding and even boast about it in times of stress on the battlefields. It would be a warm and tasty reminder of me. I took great trouble and care, not telling Chas for I wanted it to be a surprise. He sat at the dining-room table, looking all welcoming for he had remarked when coming in, 'What is that lovely smell?' I turned the pudding out on to my best oval dish and surrounded it with all the vegetables. Then singing out 'Tarah, tarah', or some such piping tune, I entered the dining-room and his eyes lit up. 'Gosh,' he said, 'that looks marvellous.' Confidence overwhelming me I swung the dish round in the manner of a professional chef, my heel caught on the carpet and the whole dish shot up in the air. I screamed with distress, then in the commotion which followed I wondered vaguely why the pudding had bounced instead of smashing to pieces. Chas looked a little puzzled too as we rescued it. He cut it with a large carving-knife and then I thought he would stab me, he was so annoyed. The pudding was just solid, no gravy or meat, the crust had turned the pudding into a large solid dumpling filled with little streaks of brown substance.

My tears did not soften Chas's disappointment or heighten his enjoyment of the bread and cheese he was forced to eat. Chas said what annoyed him as much as his disappointment was the fact that I remarked on discovering the solidity of the pudding, 'Well, dear, you wouldn't have been able to eat it if it had been perfectly made, for it would have been smashed on the floor and all the lovely gravy and meat would have been wasted.' Anyway I did give him my ration of cheese.

Most days Chas would arrive home round about late lunchtime, having completed the collection part of his duties, and even though money was extremely tight I would try to give him one real meal in the middle of the day, though I never attempted steak and kidney pudding again. It was possible to get a chop (of a sort) for 6*d.* and with this I would cook all the vegetables he grew, plus a Yorkshire pudding, so that a small chop with cauliflower, white sauce, carrots, onions etc., and a 'high-rise' Yorkshire pudding would look a meal fit for a king, plus a sweet of some sort to follow. Amy lived not far away in a new semi-detached house she and James were purchasing, at Goodmayes.

Her son Rodney was at school and her small daughter Angela not yet of school age. Compared to the rest of the family Amy was the affluent one, always such a wizard with her needle, and material and other accessories being reasonably priced in that area in those days, she always looked like a picture from *Vogue*. Sometimes she would make frocks for Angela and herself of identical material and pattern so that they could have been taken for fashion models of 'mother and daughter'. Amy also possessed a close friend of the same age, also not hard up, also with the same flair for clothes and possessing an attractive slim figure, as our Amy did. They were, to put it mildly, something to be seen and marvelled at, especially by my 'piano-divining' neighbour.

The trouble with possessing these talents and acquisitions is there is not much point in hiding their lights under a bushel, and housework completed at lunchtime, Amy, with small daughter, and friend would call on 'Dolly' each afternoon to share a dish of tea, and of course, my baby was naturally an attraction. I would hope Chas had finished his midday meal so that I could at least wash up and tidy the kitchen before these two 'ladies' arrived. I always felt like a fat slovenly matron in their company, ashamed of the pile of baby washing waiting for ironing, and my old maternity frock gathered gathered round me with a belt to give it a few fashionable gathers.

One day they arrived before I had time to wash the dinner things for Chas had been late home. The kitchen seemed full to capacity with dirty saucepans, dishes, a rice-pudding dish soaking because of the hard brown bits round the edges, a large Yorkshire pudding tin, also soaking on another table, piles of clothes from the line, ready for folding, me untidy, hot, not belted up properly in my afternoon fashion. 'Mother and daughter' and friend swept through the kitchen to go into the garden to say 'hallo' to Susan in her pram. They look absolutely fantastic, with white silk, blue spotted frocks, smart straw hats with matching bands, navy blue accessories and they carried dainty shopping baskets. Amy gazed around the kitchen with a look of utter distaste. I knew how she felt for it is very depressing to call for a cup of tea and a chat to find one's hostess 'unprepared' to say the least of it. Irritation overcame her and she said indignantly to me, 'Why do you make yourself such a lot of work, Dolly, giving Chas such a meal each day?' Then she added, gazing at the Yorkshire pudding tin with its overflowing contents of cold, pudding-spotted water, 'And Yorkshire pudding too,' just as though it was caviar!

She then swept out into the garden. Behind me stood little Angela and Amy's silent friend, the friend trying to look as though the clouds were not rising up on my domestic horizon. Bravely, I waited until Amy was out of earshot, or I thought she was, and then I said, 'Well, some people would eat . . .' (Over the years my descriptive word, which I admit was unforgivably vulgar, has altered in our memories. To me the word becomes milder and more acceptable, to Amy the word becomes more vulgar and more unacceptable.) Perhaps I was braver, or more hurt than I thought, for Amy heard my remark and assumed I was hinting that (because her sweet husband never minded, or complained about any dish set before him) she was not conscientious or interested in what she supplied at her table. Her eyes flashed, she looked so furious I trembled inwardly. She came back into the kitchen, said, 'Come, Angela' (my little niece looked so disappointed for she loved to be with Auntie Dolly), and swept out of the house. Her friend was trapped between me and the kitchen door for the kitchen was a long oblong affair. Her friend was not brave enough to say good-bye to me, and hanging her head in embarrassment she scuttled after Amy.

I knew Amy would not speak to me for a long time, if ever, and I did not intend to make the first move, but I was not courageous enough to face her head-on again until I knew how she felt. If I saw her at the shops I would dash down a side turning. I would call on Agnes for family news, praying Amy would not appear. The trouble with our family has always been that sides are taken with the 'member' present at the time. Agnes was always sympathetic to my side of the affair, but I knew she would be just as sympathetic when Amy was there with her. She hated any bad feeling and was worried we would both meet at her house before our tempers were cooled.

Finally I called on Agnes one day just as Amy was leaving. 'Hallo,' I said, just as though we'd only left each other moments before. Amy was pleased I had spoken, but I knew she was still unforgiving. She looked at Susan in her pram and said to me, 'She looks very pale, isn't she well?' which was true retribution for she knew how I worried abnormally over my baby.

But James had the last word and at last made Amy laugh. One day after visiting me when Marjorie was there, and having a happy time, she arrived home after James. He knew she had been visiting us and he said, 'And what member of your family have you upset today?'

I often wished I hadn't made that remark and listened to

Mother when she said, 'Dolly, a still tongue makes a wise head,' but I suppose it was forced from me in a mixture of shame for my untidy kitchen, and a protective feeling for my Chas, as I resented the suggestion he was not important enough for me to make an effort with his food. Or was I jealous of two ladies, more elegant than I could ever hope to be?

After a quiet spell, warfare in the air began to hot up and one day I was in the dining-room when the fireplace began to shake and make a roaring sound. In the council-houses the fires had an oven above them and the door of this oven, which opened downward, began to rattle frighteningly. At that moment the Barking guns began to boom. I had a bomb down my chimney! I threw myself on top of Susan who was crawling on the floor and waited for the explosion and I waited and waited and still the oven shook, and still we were safe, yet I daren't stand up, all the instructions said, 'Lie down.' Then there was a furious banging on the front door. I grabbed Susan and ran. There was my sallow-faced neighbour. 'It's a funny thing to set your chimney on fire when there is a raid on,' she said suspiciously. I suppose now (because I was piano-less) she thought I must be a spy. I really don't know how the chimney caught fire for my fire was only a normal one, but I was in my neighbour's bad books again, and this gave her great pleasure.

As Chas was waiting to be called to the forces, and eventually hand over his job with the Prudential to me, he was made a 'supernumerary' and took on the job of training the new lady agent as each man was called up. I was his first pupil and possibly the least conscientious of any. Marjorie, my youngest sister, was expecting her first baby, and would take care of Susan in the country. Marjorie's husband, Alfred, was already in the forces and Chas had obtained for Marjorie through the auspices of his relatives in Suffolk, a cottage, one of a pair, in a quiet country lane (which seemed to lead nowhere) at Somerton, near the pretty village of Hartest. The cottage was next to a lovely grey church which looked ghost-like as though it had no human worshippers. The cottage garden, looking out on to lush meadows, was lovely. Water had to be fetched from a pump some way distant from the cottage, quite a difficult task for Marjorie, large with child, and with Susan barely able to walk. The girl next door was friendly but out at work all day so that Marjorie had no one to speak to for weeks on end and at night time when Susan was in bed Marjorie must have felt very frightened alone in the lamp-light. The lane was overhung with trees, beautiful but darkly sad, a lonely sanctuary for them both.

Chas was determined, if it was humanly possible, to make me an efficient agent. I liked the people and was so pleased when the children ran to greet me like an old friend. But I was terrified of the dogs and when Chas gave me a 'trial run' he was horrified at my reason for so many 'non-payments'. 'Oh, the dog in that house looked so fierce.' He had to go round again 'to keep me straight'. He tried to instruct me in the art of chatting up people. 'Take the money first, then chat afterwards,' he would say, but of course I got terribly delayed, for the woman of the house and I would start talking as soon as the door was opened.

And I missed my baby so much I felt like half a person. I couldn't keep my mind on anything else really, although I tried. One day after Chas and I had had a fierce argument in a Dagenham road I tore off to the station and went down to Somerton to Marjorie for a few days. It was sheer heaven. We were all delirious at our reunion. I didn't worry about Chas's food because by that time we had two evacuees billeted on us by the authorities, a widow and her daughter, and I knew that Chas would be ensured of 'home comforts'. The widow, Mrs Beadle, was like something out of Charles Dickens. She'd had a hard life and was always referring to the 'late Mr Beadle'. He was 'very respectable' as indeed she was. Her daughter was a girl of about eighteen, tall, slim, very pale, with dark brown eyes and masses and masses of black ringlets. She worked in the City somewhere and spent her evenings off getting ready for our evening dive down into the Anderson shelter in the garden. She would do her hair up in 'crackers', pieces of rag wound round and round each ringlet. These she would dampen with spit, while she was reading a paper magazine. She seemed quite contented with her lot. Mrs Beadle, I think, worked as a charwoman somewhere and would arrive home at lunchtime when she would prepare her daughter's evening meal and put it on a saucepan to keep warm for hours until her daughter, June's, return in the evening.

They were no bother at all and Chas felt so sorry for them having to live in someone else's home that the curtailing of our love life seemed the least of our worries. Finally I became a fully fledged agent for Chas was called up for his army medical. He arrived back in a triumphant state. Baring his chest he announced, 'I've received my first medal.' On his chest over his heart was a blue circle. The doctor had discovered that Chas had an abnormal heart-beat and after eliciting from Chas the information that, no, he'd never felt faint, no, he'd not had rheumatic fever, he ordered him to chase, stripped, round the examination room at full gallop several times, after which he tested Chas's heart each time and looked dubious about accepting him at all. Eventually a delighted Chas 'received the King's shilling' and the medical grading of B1. I was furious, because if he had not been accepted I could have been in the country with Susan. He thought me most unpatriotic and asked if I wanted him to be different from other men and shirk his duty. 'Yes,' I snapped, and we went sadly to bed, knowing that 'I would not love thee half as much' did really apply to him. Once a boy scout always a boy scout I felt. I was really being incredibly selfish but I hated the thought of trudging the roads of Dagenham and coming home to an empty house, for God knew how long. Now, too, I knew about Chas's peculiar heart I would be more worried by the hard times I knew our men would have.

On the day of his departure we crawled out of the shelter, aching from our makeshift bed and the damp atmosphere. It was still dark but Chas was so anxious not to be late 'on parade'. An air raid was in progress but neither of us seemed unduly perturbed about this. He said good-bye to the Beadles who broke down and cried and Chas cleared his throat noisily. As we went out into the cold and dismal road the guns seemed suddenly ear-splitting and I suggested we go back into the shelter and wait for the all-clear. 'You go, dear,' said Chas, 'But I have a train to catch,' and in a state of nightmarish numbness I took his arm. How could I be less brave (or stupid I felt) than this obstinate man with his innate sense of duty? It seemed, when we reached the main line station, that I was the only cowardly one, for the platform was teeming with men accompanied by sad wives and mothers. Some were crying and I felt guilty that I couldn't squeeze even one tear. I just wanted the train to come in and go out with all speed possible. I was so cold I felt as though I was frozen to the ground, like a statue that has lost its plinth.

Chas hardly kissed me good-bye as though he was eager to be gone and I smiled brightly as I waved him good-bye. I almost said, 'Have a good time,' as though he was going on holiday. I wondered if he felt me callous, a happy-looking wife amongst so many weeping women, but he wrote me that he would always remember my lovely smiling face as the train left the station. He said if I had broken down he would have wept in sympathy. He added, 'You are my brave soldier girl,' which undeserved compliment made me feel extremely guilty.

'Don't worry, gel,' said my father. 'He'll have a fine time in the army, and what's more, it'll make a man of him.' I thought this a two-edged remark but I believed my father implicitly and I looked forward to my darling returning, not the pale-faced worried young man I had waved off, but a giant, tanned, smiling and muscular.

Having made himself useful to the Sergeant (by typing for him in his spare time) Chas arrived home after his training period before the other recruits. Excitedly I met him at the station, and what a sorry sight met my eyes. Where was the new manly Chas my father had insisted I would meet? His eye was black and his face bruised, and he seemed more bent than the weight of his pack was responsible for. It transpired that they were drilling one day in a rather confined space. He was in the row behind an abnormally short recruit. As the order came to slope arms, up came this midget's gun (and he was a very strong dwarf) right into Chas's eye knocking him unconscious. He sprained his back too. 'Lucky for you it wasn't fixed bayonets,' I said—a remark I thought he took in the wrong spirit. In addition to these troubles he had an enormous carbuncle at the base of his spine because he was allergic to one of the inoculations. This had been lanced, and eager to get home, he had assured the M.O. his wife would be happy and competent to dress this.

Chas had had no experience of my bravery under fire, or my cowardice at the sight of blood. My mother, who was visiting, could have told him but she just gave us both a strange look and went off to the shops. After a quick cup of tea I scrubbed up, Chas dropped his trousers and I gazed in horror at the wound on his spine. I had assured myself I would be a gentle and efficient nurse, making up to him for all my shortcomings. I loved him dearly and had always understood that love conquers all, but suddenly I had a far away feeling and an unspoken fear that love, in my case, was not strong enough to dress this carbuncled gash. At an earlier scene of cowardice the doctor had said, 'Put your head between your legs,' and I turned round from my husband, and back to back we bowed in homage to the floor, me praying for courage, he wondering, 'What kept you?' He hadn't taken his trousers off for he had faith in my speedy ministrations and it crossed my mind to wonder why men look all right in shorts but so absurd with their trousers round their ankles. 'Ready,' I said brightly, just like my 'rub it well in' Matron, but as I caught sight of his septic spine for the second time, again I felt as though I would pass out. Chas, fed up with bending like a praying mantis, straightened up, and when he saw my face, which must have been green he said, 'Oh, my poor love, why didn't you tell me you were ill? Here, let me help you to the sofa.' We hobbled, at least he hobbled, I was dragged to the sofa and he then hobbled off to the kitchen for some water. I was so ashamed of myself I was determined to succour this brave and uncomplaining man, so we tried again. After my third fainting-fit he would allow no more Florence Nightingale attempts, he said he would manage himself, but my mother who had returned and was hovering in the hall outside, having given Dolly enough time to 'do her duty', decided it was time to enter the 'surgery', came to the rescue and dressed the wound. I knew my mother was ashamed of me, indeed I was ashamed of myself. Chas was full of apologies to me which made me feel more abject. He was brave, the Scannells and the Chegwiddens were all brave, so what was it about broken flesh which made *me* the one coward amongst them? I prayed emergencies would avoid me for the rest of my life.

Chas was posted to a searchlight site in Devon and I became an efficient insurance agent, according to the Superintendent, obtaining phenomenal new business.

Very warm, very easy to get on with were my Dagenham clients. Always a cheery word, and a joke, even after a terrible night in the air-raid shelters. There is, of course, an exception everywhere, and I had one strange family on my round. Although still friendly, still offering me that cheering cup of tea, I was unable to accept, and not only because it was rationed, though that was a good excuse. When approaching this house I had to take a long deep breath, for when their door opened a foul stream of air assailed my nostrils. I could only liken it to swampy jungle ozone. And the dirt, well, it was impossible to describe. I can only say it was so dirty that it never appeared dirtier each week I called. It was so dirty that no extra dirt would have made any difference. The 'lady' of the house was tall and thin with a cloud of fair hair surrounding her face, her children too, were pale and thin. I had to go into the house once because of a claim. It was the worst experience of my life and I think really, I could have faced it, but for the dreadful stench of sheer putridity. A child was eating dry cornflakes off a filthy table, the mother was holding a frying-pan in her hand, the only piece of equipment visible in that kitchen, I think it was used for all culinary purposes. It was filled with dry black substance up to the rim of the pan. Yet had they been clean and well fed they would all have been raving beauties, they all possessed masses of cloudy fair hair, high cheek-bones, and naturally, being half-starved, enormous soulful-looking eyes. I never saw the husband but I believe he was at work and I wondered why they were as they were. The woman was 'nicely spoken', they were not illiterate. What had brought them to this degradation?

In the evenings I went back to my 'round' dressed up like a model (people didn't recognise me out of my Churchillian boiler-suit and head scarf) to canvass for new business. Various 'gentle-man' friends accompanied me, usually old stalwarts of the company, expert sellers of insurance. I would go through my 'register' beforehand to make a list of people who would, or could, or should, be given the 'opportunity' of purchasing 'extra cover'. People treated our visits as a call of honoured guests. I was popular, the children liked me, and I used to spend my time amusing the children while my companion 'did his turn', for selling bored and somewhat embarrassed me. The old stal-warts all had one line which was theirs and theirs alone. When it looked as though the people weren't quite sure whether to take out insurance or not, one representative would always say, 'Well, of course, Madam, you know your purse better than I.' Another would say, 'The choice is yours, Madam, I never persuade a lady against her will' (knowing this one, I thought, 'give him half a chance'), 'I can only advise.'

The tales these old stalwarts told me of years and years ago would shock many an insurance man of today. I wondered how they ever got round when they were young men, or ever had the strength to go home, and I wondered where the rounds had been in the 1920s, for there were no ladies on my round, starving for love, as apparently they had been in 'the good old days' of my canvasser friends. They all seemed disappointed when I went straight home after a canvassing session. I used to think, how conceited is the male, he may be old, toothless, bald, trembly (well, that's natural) and yet he always has that unfailing belief in his appeal to the opposite sex, however attractive and young the female might be.

It was lovely when I called at the houses where people had their books and correct money at the ready. Lots of women, myself included, have to turn their homes inside out searching for that elusive purse. One Monday morning I called at a house, where, without fail, business was concluded swiftly, nevertheless cheerfully, in a matter of seconds. This bright Monday morning I rat-a-tatted. Instead of the immediate opening of the door came a frantic scream from the occupant. 'Just a minute, Mrs S., I'm seeing to a snake.' Then before the words had sunk in came terrific thuds, crashes and cries from my client. Had she had a breakdown through the long separation from her husband? I wondered. Were the raids too much for her, or worse still, was she being attacked by a German spy or parachutist? I must fetch help I decided, but just as I reached the garden gate, the door opened and my name was called. The house was always immaculate, a band-box of a place. The young wife always bright and well groomed. She had cleaned the whole house that morning and was brushing the last bottom stair when she heard a swishing noise above her head. Looking up, to her horror, on the top stair was a snake, and it was weaving to and fro, just as snakes did on the films.

She had dashed into the garden for a spade and returned with it just as I knocked on her door. She was afraid that had she opened the door the snake might come out at me, or it might have crawled somewhere else in her house. She had, for her peace of mind, to know where the snake was. She had attacked the snake, killed it and before opening the door to me, had thrown it out on a heap of coal in her back garden. 'Would you have a cup of tea with me?' she said. 'I feel trembly now.' After our tea she asked if I would like to see the snake. 'If it's really dead,' was my brave reply. We went into the garden just as the cat next door slunk away. He had eaten the snake with the exception of its head and this lay evil and malevolent looking, even without its body. It was a kind of blackish yellow. It was a mystery where it had come from; in her clean house there was nowhere to hide, unless it had been coiled up somewhere on a warm boiler in the loft. My client did not think she was brave at all for she said, 'There was nothing else I could do.' I could have thought of another alternative.

I had become friendly with the Superintendent and his wife and she suggested, while Chas was away and Susan with Marjorie, that I move in with them. In this way her husband would assist me with my accounts—I was sometimes short and had to put money in at the time of my audits. No doubt I was doing what Chas had warned me I would, chatting away, entering the premiums in the books and sometimes dashing off absent-mindedly without taking the cash. The wife would see that I had regular meals and they worried about me being in an empty house during the air-raids, for the Beadles had been given accommodation by the council. The Superintendent's next-door neighbour was an engineer and between them they had built an underground shelter in the garden. It was made of stone, deep, deep down, with electric light, air-conditioning and facilities for preparing a meal. The raids seemed so distant in this shelter, safe as houses the engineer opined, but I hated every minute in it. To me it was a mausoleum, and I was happier out in the open doing my rounds, which made my friends very cross.

They were kind to me although I realised they couldn't know how I felt with my family scattered. I had never been interested in my appearance so far as elegant costume, or coiffure, was concerned and the Superintendent's wife decided I could look a striking woman if I took an interest. She was a very smart woman and decided to take me in hand. Each week we visited her hair stylist who said I would need many visits to bring my hair into line with the style he planned for me, Pompadour. My thick tresses were shorn and then thinned gradually. I was led like a lamb to the slaughter. My precious clothing coupons were squandered on a tailored suit, silk shirt, and top coat. My warm woollen vests and pants were discarded and replaced by silk panties and very soon I had the added job of repulsing the advances of older men who couldn't be called up. Now a bird of paradise and no longer in the uniform of a mourning wife, they seemed to think me fair game. The more attractive they seemed to think me the more I hated and detested them, how dare they seek my company when my husband was away at the war, especially as they knew him and liked him. I spent every moment I could in Suffolk with Marjorie and Susan, and now, her baby Richard. When I made my first visit to Marjorie after my transformation she burst into tears. She said, 'Oh, Dolly, I didn't recognise you when you came down the road, you looked like a mannequin, you haven't gone away from us, have you?' I certainly felt another person with my new plumage and loss of weight through the miles I had walked.

However, salvation came in the form of the local doctor, a down-to-earth matter-of-fact Scotsman. Flimsy silk knickers were definitely not the right garb for outdoor work in the depths of winter and I became ill with cystitis. My hostess came to the surgery with me and so heard the doctor say, 'With your job, lassie, what you need is plenty of porridge and warm trews.'

But in any case my stay at this lovely modern house was nearing its end. My benefactors possessed an elegant collie, a gentleman of a dog, beautifully trained and beautiful to look at with his lovely long fur and glowing eyes. I made friends with him, no fear of dogs now, so that when they went away for the weekend I was quite happy to be alone with Mac. One Saturday we had had a couple of air-raids, but the 'all clear' having sounded, I was tired, so went to bed. Suddenly I was awoken by a noisy barking and found Mac tugging at my bedclothes. I thought he had gone berserk for he began dragging at the sleeve of my pyjamas. I began to feel quite nervous and decided to go downstairs. Mac bounced down after me and as we reached the bottom stair there was a terrific explosion. It seemed as though there was a huge typhoon which was making the house collapse and something wet ran down my face. Then came a fierce knocking at the door and an air-raid warden enquired if I was O.K. A land-mine had come down in the next road. When the rescue squad looked at my bed they said Mac should receive a medal, for where my head would have been was a rafter from the roof, and embedded in my pillow, an enormous nail.

I wrote to Chas, glossing over the details, but hinting that perhaps it would be better for me to relinquish my job and go to Suffolk with Marjorie, for with both of us at the front line, more or less, Susan might become an orphan. My stiff upper lip decision deceived him because he took my light-hearted letter literally and advised me to 'be his brave soldier girl and stick it out'. This of course was guaranteed to put me in a catty mood, to say the least of it, especially as I took his cheerful letters literally—I thought they had fun on a winter's night on a Dartmoor searchlight site. I could not know they tried to sleep in freezing winter darkness in unlighted tents, oozing with mud, sometimes with only one blanket per man! Later, when Chas became troop clerk he obtained a *nine-inch wide wooden couch* to sleep on. One of the forms issued, 'Soldier, for the use of', on which they sat at meal-times. Of course, it was only a 'single' bed.

I began to become envious of his life and feel Susan and I were hard done by, especially after I'd read about one amusing day he'd had. On one occasion on manoeuvres, he was dressed up as a curate and accompanied by an ATS girl in civvies, the object being to spy out the land and observe 'the enemy' without being discovered. During their exercises, whilst trying to hide from the enemy, they were forced to lie together in a hedge, and cover themselves with leaves. (I was a little suspicious of this babes in the wood part.) So well were they hidden that members of the 'enemy' came and urinated upon them and Chas said, 'Do you know after that terrible experience we still never moved? Well, we wouldn't have done if they were really the enemy, would we?' I think he and his lady companion were 'highly commended'.

He also used to play tennis at the vicarage. One young lady, knowing his fondness for salads brought him lettuces and home-grown tomatoes and in one of his letters he added a postscript to the effect that if I ever had a couple of pounds spare cash lying round he would be very pleased of same. Whether it was his rabbiting on about his high-life in Devon, his humility in the way he asked for the cash, or my annoyance at the 'brave soldier girl bit', I do not know, but I dashed off a letter to him so vitriolic in its content that I was not surprised at his awful reply in return. Divorce! Of course I calmed down and poured oil on troubled waters by sending him a whole five pounds! I imagine I begrudged it for I was saving hard for his return. The Prudential were absolutely marvellous to the wives of their serving agents for they made up their soldier's allowance, which was small, so I received full wages for Chas each month. In addition to this my wages were good and I earned lots of commission. We had never been so well off in our lives. Eventually our letters got back to normal.

Then Susan became very ill with whooping-cough and complications and I left the Superintendent's house, went back to my flat at Forest Gate and brought Susan home from the country to be with me. The doctor suggested Chas try to get a few days' compassionate leave and I sent a certificate to Chas but he replied that he couldn't show this to the authorities because he felt as whooping-cough was a contagious disease it wouldn't be fair to his 'buddies' some of whom had their wives and children in Devon. I still carried on with my job for Chas's sister came over during the day to be with Susan, but one night I was alone with baby in the cellar when she had a convulsion and I felt it was better to chance the bombs and be upstairs with her in the warm for the cold musty cellar couldn't be doing her any good. My parents were in Wales with my sister Winifred but as soon as they heard I was back at Forest Gate with a sick baby they took the next train back, and Susan seemed to recover rapidly.

My father was delighted to be in the front line again and was extremely daring, much to Mother's annoyance and distress. He would just not take cover during the raids. At the time of the incendiary bombs he would be on the prowl all round the house and garden watching for them with his little stirrup-pump. He was so foolhardy and obstinate he wouldn't even wear a tin hat. Because he remained unscathed during the greater part of the war he convinced himself, I think, that he bore a charmed life, so that when he was finally 'wounded' it was entirely due to his own foolhardiness. Later in the war, at the time of the doodlebugs, he was in his bedroom upstairs. He had the window open and was hanging perilously out watching one of these fiery puffing trains in the sky wondering where and when its engines would 'cut out'. Mother, worried as to where he was, had noiselessly entered the bedroom. She had a way of gliding very quietly, rather like those long-plaited Russian dancers. She reached Father just as the engines of the doodlebug ceased preparatory to its terrible dive to earth, and saying in loud tones, 'Whatever are you doing, Walter, hanging out of the window when the doodlebug is ready to drop?' She put her hand on his shoulder. He had been unaware of her approach and started back from the window in fright at her voice and the approaching calamity above him. As he did so Mother's teeth collided with his bald head. Her two front teeth were knocked out and he had a nasty bite in the middle of his crown. 'Strike me pink, woman, what are you bleeding well creeping about for?' he shouted. But when I arrived home he was laughing about it and I thought my mother looked very comical with her two front teeth missing, even though she may not have felt as jocular as she looked.

Susan became ill again and it was then I decided to stay home and care for her, and in spite of the severe raids, the time she and I spent with my parents at Forest Gate was a really happy one. My father played with Susan for hours and their 'favourite' game was tea-parties. One wet day I was out queuing for fish, a luxury, for it wasn't on the ration and so no food coupons were needed. It was a long wait, for the queue formed before the fish arrived. Dad said he would take care of Susan while Mother popped next door to visit a sick neighbour. On Mother's return she was horrified to find her dining-room floor swimming with water. 'Oh, Dad,' she wailed. 'Why ever did you give Susan water to play with in here?' 'I never gave Susan any water,' insisted an indignant grandfather, 'We've just been having a tea-party. I've drunk *twenty-four* cups of delicious "tea", the best I have ever tasted, haven't I, Susie?' Mother didn't believe my father, for she knew Susan couldn't reach the taps and she asked

Susan to show her where the water came from. Susan took mother's hand, led her to the bathroom and pointed to the lavatory-pan.

My father, horrified on discovering the true identity of the 'delicious' tea, screamed out, 'Strike me bloody hooray!', grabbed his cap and tore off at full speed to the chemist, deciding that rhubarb pills, nature's cure of his earlier days, would save him from fatal poisoning. On arriving home he swallowed more than double the dose and Mother said in an indignant and injured tone, 'I don't know why you are making all this fuss, Walter, my lavatory-pan *is clean.*' The next day our tea-taster was quite poorly. Naturally he blamed the 'tea-water' and not the rhubarb pills.

One of my temporary jobs after my marriage, had been working for Sun Maid Raisins and there I met a charming man, Walter, who lived nearby at Stratford so that it was not surprising that I should bump into him one day. He was then working with a friend who had acquired a wholesale fish merchants in Billingsgate and as they were busy and required a secretary he introduced me to his friend, the owner. Mr Mitchell, Walter's friend, was also a charming man and I worked there happily for some time. Fearing that caring for Susan might be too much for my parents, although they had never said so, I found a nursery school for her at Stratford. After a few days my father insisted that Susan was unhappy at this school and when I discovered my parents walked to the school every afternoon and always saw Susan alone in the little playground, sitting in a corner sucking her thumb, I gave in and let them take care of her. Certainly the three of them seemed always very happy at this arrangement. Whenever possible my employer let me have some fish, even if only enough for Susan, so that my working at Billingsgate helped us with the difficult task of making our rations last.

Fortunately Susan always had her pint of milk daily for she was under five years of age. It was really a question of eking the rations out. Mother had never shopped here and there but always at the same grocers and butchers etc. so sometimes this helped when there was offal about. Father planted potatoes etc. in the back garden and somehow we managed for I was able to queue up for things off the ration and in short supply because I knew Susan was well looked after at home with my parents. My father grew spinach, which seemed everlasting, and although I hated it I swallowed it with chips when we had a little fat to spare for frying. Of course four people could manage better on four ration-books than one person could with one ration-book.

I queued up nearly the whole of one day at the Town Hall when parcels were sent from America for old-age pensioners. An excited Mother looked at the presentation bag I brought home, $1\frac{1}{2}$ lb. of cooking fat—and it was rancid! I suppose it had been so long in coming. I think we still used it for chips!

I must have been the only female at Billingsgate, I feel, for I was the centre of attraction every morning on arrival. I had to ascend a wrought-iron spiral staircase to the office above the market and I found this difficult to negotiate respectably. Skirts were a bit shorter then, a sort of war-time economy, although by today's standards they were a modest calf-length being just below the knee. I had to hold my bag and also hold my skirt down while climbing these giddy-making stairs which had patterned holes in them. My ascent was always a focal-point for male concentration each morning.

On my first morning there a porter asked me if I would like 'elevenses', and I accepted eagerly his offer of tea and a slice of bread and dripping. He arrived back from the café and placed on my desk, well it wasn't even a mug, it was a white china pail, full to the brim with strong, very strong, red tea. Round the edge of the 'cup' was a ring of fingerprints, bloody and scaly. The two slices of bread and dripping were each the thickness of a third of a loaf and these were wrapped in newspaper bearing the same fish scales and red smears. I seem to remember the whole 'meal' cost only 3*d*. But, of course, this rich repast was not for me and ever after I made the office elevenses myself.

CHAPTER EIGHT

The Court Martial

I should have realised that to make plans, even in one's mind, was stupid during war-time, and the raids got so terrible that Mother began to worry for Susan's safety and she prevailed on me to take Susan down into Suffolk with Marjorie and Richard until the intensity of the bombing lessened. I would have liked my parents to have left Forest Gate also, but my father was a front-line soldier, he loved his home, the danger, to him, was less painful than having to live in someone else's house, even though that someone else was a daughter.

I was deeply shocked at Marjorie's appearance. She had changed from a bright, attractive, healthy-looking girl into a thin, worried, delicate-looking woman. Living in the peace and plenty of the countryside I expected to see her blooming. Of course I hadn't realised that because she was only receiving a small army allowance she had been forced to find a job. Her allotment had been increased to about 27*s.* when her baby had been born and the doctor advised her to apply for extra as she couldn't work with a baby to care for. An old chap had arrived to enquire into her circumstances, rather an aggressive type Marjorie felt, and because she had no debts or hire purchase payments she was granted an extra 2*s.* per week! This hurt her pride and she returned it to the authorities and obtained a job in the local bakehouse. The hot bakehouse and heavy equipment soon took the bloom from her cheeks and she lost an enormous amount of weight.

So, for once, Dolly rose to the occasion and in this emergency took charge. Marjorie gave up her job and I became the man of the house. I painted and decorated the country cottage, stained the floors, and made the place look all chintzy, and even with my cooking Marjorie gradually began to be her old self again. I knew she felt better the day she ticked me off for using the cabbage saucepan for potatoes. To me saucepans were saucepans, indeed how could I tell the difference, they looked exactly alike. I never separated my own saucepans for different cookings, but to Marjorie, ever fussy, this was a culinary crime.

I became the inventor of new dishes although in my case necessity was the mother of invention. We had run out of ration-book rations one day. Marjorie and the children would be coming home for the evening meal, literally starving for the weather was crisp and cold, just the sort of day to give one an appetite. I was at my wits' end when one of Chas's old uncles called with the present of a large marrow. Now I detested marrow, but during a war sometimes detested commodities become life-savers. I peeled and de-gutted the marrow and stuffed it with everything I could find, grated cheese rinds, carrots, onions, parsnips, swede, all minced up and mixed with some 'gravy' I discovered at the bottom of a cup of dripping. I tied it up like a 'cock-a-trice' and roasted it with potatoes and cauliflower. It was voted the best meal in years, so I knew the family must have been very hungry.

We took the children skating on the pond in a real snowy country scene just like a postcard, except that bruises are not shown in those idyllic scenes, nor red noses, nor children crying with frozen fingers. We went nutting, blackberrying, picnicking, and once, when Chas was on leave, gleaning. He had enjoyed this so much as a small boy in Suffolk that he took a dim view of our complaints of stubble-torn legs. But it was impossible to shut out the war for ever and my return to the 'front line' came in the shape of a communication from the Bank Manager. It was my first bank account and although I had written cheques for my needs, I never dreamt I was living a Micawber-type life. The letter pronounced that I was £84 'in the red', and an early settlement would be appreciated. 'I'm £84 in the red,' I announced to Marjorie, feeling in need of another's sympathy and advice. 'Oh, Dee,' said Marjorie. 'Is that good?'

There was nothing for it but to go back to work. The only employment locally appeared to be the bakehouse or a clothing factory which was some miles away, and always hopeless with my needle and terrified at the thought of a sewing-machine, I decided to return to Forest Gate and Billingsgate. After all, from my safe vantage-point in the country I felt I could face a few bombs, my memory of the damage caused by these fiendish contraptions had become somewhat blurred. Susan and I were happy to be home again with my parents and life resumed much as it was before.

Until the day I took a telephone-call from Chas, now in the wilds of Scotland. He had an unexpected thirty-six hours' leave, and could get home for one night. I was excited about this unexpected treat but a little worried that the result might be an addition to our family. It definitely was not the right time for such indulgences and I knew Chas, miles from any chemists, would be unprepared. I decided I must be the girl guide. There was no one I could ask about this matter, certainly not my parents, they had never made such criminal purchases. Then I remembered passing, in Ilford High Road, a private clinic which supplied such necessities. I remembered, too, that there were, blessed salvation, two entrances, 'Ladies' and 'Gentlemen'. On arriving in Ilford I walked up and down the road for a long time, not only plucking up courage to enter, but also making sure that I would meet none of my old insurance-agent friends, for what would they have thought? Mine was definitely not a usual feminine errand. At last I entered the 'Ladies' door of this luxurious-looking clinic, expecting to be met by a female nurse, or even lady doctor.

I was rehearsing the words with which I would enquire, casually, for my purchase, when I realised that the counter stretched the whole width of the 'clinic' (in reality, a 'shop'). The 'clinic' was divided from the 'Ladies' and 'Gentlemen's' entrance door by a wooden partition which was only my height from the floor, so that inside the clinic there was no real segregation of the sexes. Not that I was worried a male customer would leap this partition, but I felt it unfair and cheating because from the road outside a lady would have every right to assume that her delicate, or indelicate, mission would be confidential. Had there been a male customer present I would have fled for ever, but I was alone in the clinic and prepared to meet my lady assistant. An inner door opened and a white overalled MAN! approached me. To his 'Yerss, Moddom?' I stammered out the word 'Sheath', assuming he'd pass me a little paper packet so I could rush away for ever. But he said, 'What quality, madam?' I couldn't answer and he said gently, 'Perhaps you'd like silk finish, madam, I'll show you some samples,' and he turned round to the walls which I now observed were lined with dark blue drawers bearing little gold handles. It was just like Oxenham's the draper's shop of my childhood. He placed on the counter four of these enormous drawers, all filled to capacity with hundreds and hundreds of 'you know what'. Just as I was about to say, 'I'll take one of those' a male customer appeared on the other side of the half-barrier. He was a florid-looking man wearing a bowler-hat at a rakish angle, and sporting gold teeth, waxed moustache, spotted handkerchief in pocket, walking stick with a gold knob, and a look of 'come hither, darling, I see you've got the goods!'

I turned my back to this Romeo and decided to say quickly and professionally to the white-coated man, 'I'll take a quarter of a dozen of these.' I proffered some silver, but my release did not come. To my utter horror and humiliation and great joy from the gold-knobbed man, the assistant approached a little gold tap on the wall. On this he fixed one of my purchases and suddenly it became an enormous balloon. I felt I should faint whilst waiting for the bang—three bangs! As the third deflation took place I assumed my release was at hand, but still worse was to come. The assistant approached me with what appeared in my demented state to be a brass carrot, and powdering the deflations he fitted them on to the carrot, one by one, and for three tormented years, it seemed years to me, he worked this carrot backwards and forwards, all the while chatting to the waiting male and me. I must have looked apoplectic for he said, 'Warm weather for this time of the year, don't you think, Modom?' I staggered from the 'clinic' and hurried to the bus stop. On the way I noticed a queue outside a tobacconists. They had cigarettes! I had given up smoking as a war-time measure but I took my turn on the queue and hurried to a little side street where I inhaled, with great relief, a De Reszke Minor. I was met by a sad mother when I got home. Chas's leave had been cancelled! Suddenly I hated all men.

Chas and I had been unable to 'talk things over' before he left for warmer climes for his departure to the front had been an unexpected nightmarish shock in the middle of the night. He was stationed in Scotland with men of a similar low medical category. Rumour had it, very strong rumour, that they were to be trained for taking charge of Southern Eastern Command when we invaded France. Naturally, being a man conscious of 'careless talk costs lives', he had not cheered me up by telling me of this near-certainty rumour. True they had 'dummy-runs' at dawn and pre-dawn, and indeed at any time of the day or night. They were issued with tropical kit, 'eskimo' kit, received all known inoculations, but, although, naturally, inoculations cannot be withdrawn, the various types of kit were withdrawn, so that the men sure of their place on British soil for the duration, assumed that these 'manoeuvres' were to fox any fifth columnists who might be lurking in Scotland.

One morning they were awoken in the dark at 3 o'clock. 'Another bloody pantomime,' said one chap. Off they went on another routine march, again they piled into a train on the small Scottish station. Off they went to sleep. Suddenly, Freddie, one of their number, yelled out, 'Christ, look at this bloody great ship.' The others didn't open their eyes, he was the practical joker. 'Shut up, you silly great sod,' said his best chum kindly. 'Let's get a bit of shut-eye.' But Freddie was too excited now. 'Look, Ron,' he yelled, 'There's a load of American G.I.s waving to me.' The carriage, now awake, felt their hearts beating. There *was* a great ship, there *were* thousands of men, American and British soldiers, going up the gang-plank, in and out of sheds, and in a cold, wet, Scottish dawn they tumbled out of the train to commence their first 'sea cruise'. It was afternoon before they finally got on to the boat. (It was the *Durban Castle* and I was 'told' years later that it carried 6000 men on that voyage!)

We usually worked later than the Market staff so that Billingsgate was very quiet when the siren went one day in 1944. As the roof was entirely of glass Mr M insisted we should go down to the shelter for we could hear the ominous chug chug of a doodlebug (a pilotless aircraft!). We stood outside a gas decontamination shelter which had just been erected and watched the doodlebug as it motor-biked its way above us towards the buildings in King William Street, willing it to reach the river, but when it was overhead its engines cut out and in the ominous silence we three dived into the shelter. The explosion that followed partially demolished the shelter but we were only a little scratched though covered from head to foot in a sort of coarse grey powder (disintegrated breeze-blocks). As we made our way out of the shelter, Walter, always courteous and charmingly mannered, held out his hand to assist me over the rubble. As he did so he clutched hold of what appeared to be a hanging lavatory-chain and a stream of water poured down over him.

What a sight met our eyes when we arrived back in the office. Mr Mitchell had just completed the modernisation of the office. It had looked lovely, very American and elegant, but now it was an absolute wreck. In addition, fish had been blown up from the market and were lying in dusty and awkward positions everywhere, even on the mantelpiece and light brackets. I gazed at the three of us, like occupants of Mars, covered in grey dust, Walter streaky from his shower, Mr Mitchell's face a picture of tragic misery at the sight of his lovely office, and I started to laugh. Mr Mitchell had always seemed such a calm man I was surprised he got very cross with me, but of course I deserved it. Possibly his annoyance helped him to relieve *his* tension.

I decided that two lucky escapes was all I could expect during the war and again I took Susan to Suffolk.

The question of work now became an urgent matter. Susan was admitted to the little village school so that I should be free all day. Richard, Marjorie's little boy, was still too young to go even though the village schoolmistress helped mothers by taking the children earlier than normal. So it was decided if I could get a job somewhere my contribution to the housekeeping would enable Marjorie to stay at home and look after us all. On our walks through the countryside I had noticed some building activity in the grounds of a large country mansion. I discovered, on enquiry, that it was to be a hospital for American wounded. I went to the Labour Exchange in the nearby market town and through them obtained the position as secretary to an American Major, Milton J. Goldsmith. He was very sorry I had obtained the position through the Labour Exchange, for had I enquired at the hospital I would have been employed by the Americans under the lend-lease arrangement and received double the wages I did get. Although financially unlucky, it did not detract from my happy time there.

I felt, at first, a bit of a traitor working for the Americans, even though they were our allies. I felt I should really be working for the British forces, not only because I was receiving the British rate of pay, but because the British soldier was hard up compared with the Americans, and that hardly made for good relations between the two sides. Not that there was any open hostility, but there was no real social mixing at first between them. Indeed among the natives it was said of the Americans, 'Overpaid, Oversexed and Over here', but I was always their staunch defender, although I understood how 'our boys' felt. For one thing the feminine choice veered towards the Americans; one might say, they had so much more to give.

Milton J., my American, was a huge man with dark curly hair and an intensely shy manner. He hadn't been married very long and was very proud of his bride back in the States. I worked in a very hot Nissen hut with about sixty service men and Milton J. The first day I took dictation from him he signed some of the letters and was then called away. As all the letters he had signed had been word perfect, I assumed it was in order for me to sign the rest on his behalf. I was very pleased with myself for translating them so well for he had a strong American twang and dictated at great speed.

The next morning when I entered the Nissen hut to start work I was greeted by sixty American soldiers barking, whining and howling like dogs. The noise was incredible. I had heard them the day before discussing another soldier, saying, 'Gee, he's a wolf,' and here was I faced with sixty wolves. Milton J. wasn't in the hut when the telephone rang. I lifted the phone, gave the name of the department, and there was actually another dog crying, barking and howling on the other end of the line. Then Milton J. arrived, laughing. At the end of all the letters I had signed I had typed what I thought Milton J. had dictated in his American twang 'Towser'. It was perfectly obvious to me it was a code name to fox the enemy. Apparently it should have been E.T.O.U.S.A. (European Theatre of Operations, United States Army). Hence the howling. What an army I had got myself into. For ever after I was called Towser, but I had, through my innocent mistake, gained the reputation of having a great sense of humour, and from then on any remark of mine was greeted with more hilarity than I sometimes felt it deserved.

Marjorie and I once went for a walk with two G.I.s to meet the children from a party the troops gave for the local children. We weren't quite sure of the route and at one time thought we were lost. 'You couldn't get lost in a little country like England, Dee,' said Marjorie. 'No,' I countered, 'but we might get DElayed for a couple of days.' Neither Marjorie nor I found this funny but the men were in hysterics and this remark was repeated all over the camp.

To add to my notoriety I was voted the girl 'with the most terrific gams' on the camp. I honestly don't think there was much competition and since the prize for the winner was a week-end in 'Cole-Chester' with the G.I. of my choice, I thought it was hardly worth winning. However, I've often wondered since what I missed by refusing such a prize!

News of my famous 'gams' having spread, the office was continuously visited by 'messengers' coming to the 'wrong' department bearing the wrong messages. Milton J. thought they were coming to compare the merchandise with Betty Grable, and he decided the Nissen hut should be made into a private office for us so that we could get on with our work. Unfortunately, or perhaps unfortunately for some, war-time economy allowed only half walls and doors to Major J. and his secretary's sanctum so that I thought it looked a little bit like a large French lavatory. The walls came down only to my knees so that my gams were open for inspection all day long without the major knowing. Although outwardly modestly disdaining my premier position legs-wise, I was secretly a little bit pleased and took to wearing nylons to enhance my prancing legs, and there was no shortage of these. It was almost an admission price to the hospital.

As I gained an unsought-after reputation, by accident, I also gained a reputation for efficiency. After all, a new typist, doing unusual work, who could cope with everything, and still crack an unexpected joke, she must be extra-efficient, or so they thought. But one evening, as I was leaving, the Major hurried after me. I was detailed, the next morning, to take a shorthand report at a Court Martial. I could hardly sleep that night, there was no point in praying that the official military recorder would return, he was abroad on an urgent mission. My shorthand was adequate, but I was no Court reporter. I prayed that the prisoner might escape, and I had nightmares when I thought of the muddle I had got into in my single life at a court of enquiry as to a fire at a London bus depot. But that seemed simple now for I had had someone to help me sort it all out afterwards. Here I would be with American Brass Hats. How could I ask them, 'What did he say then?' I could have stayed home with a bilious attack but a jeep was to call for me. Perhaps *I* would be arrested if I failed to appear.

At least, I thought, I shall be well garbed. When I had worked as an insurance agent I had become friendly with one of my customers, a middle-aged, ruddy-looking woman, cockney, hail-fellow-well-met. She had invited me in for a cup of tea. She was making a bread pudding, a gigantic affair, using the washing-up bowl for the bread from which she was squeezing the water. Every now and then she would remove a long hair from the mixture! She asked me if I liked bread pudding and my answer was gently negative. Now she said she had always admired my classy manner and could tell I was from a nice home, like a clergyman's. (Perhaps that is why my old Dagenham neighbour was sure I should have a piano, or an organ!) She had, she said, a Harris tweed costume which was 'just me'. It was only £3. She brought out this costume, which was new, and genuine Harris tweed, one of those gingery ones that blue-blooded ladies used for country walking or shooting in. Clothes coupons being very tight I bought the suit, thinking it a bit strange when she advised me to 'hide it somewhere' because of the neighbours. On my next call in addition to a marvellous brown pinafore-dress in wool georgette she had a quantity of real shantung blouses, and a dark-haired young man whom she introduced as 'her lodger'. He was very handsome and very sleepy.

Now I began to be worried. I took the pinafore-dress and a lovely shantung blouse, but told her I could not have anything else because I had to send all my money into the country for my baby. I felt dreadful, my husband was fighting and his wife was acting against the war effort. I began to wish the lady would move, but one day she called me in for advice. She was pregnant! Was it the handsome young lodger, or her husband? I was astounded that the handsome young lodger could have desired my client, but she said it only happened because she had gone into the sitting-room straight after her bath! I can't remember advising her to 'come clean' and confess to her husband but within a few weeks lodger, lady, children and husband were gone from the district, and sadly I heard they were killed in an air-raid.

I would wear the brown pinafore-dress and shantung blouse to the Court Martial. There were a few wolf whistles as I went into our Nissen hut the next morning to collect my pad and pencil. A Sergeant sharpened it at both ends for me. I asked him if a man was guilty of a serious crime whether he was shot in war-time, if he was not at the battle-front. 'Oh, yes, Towser,' he said. 'You'll be in at the shooting so be careful what you take down.' My colleagues laughed as I left the hut and I arrived trembling at the Court. It was held in a building attached to the main hospital. There were two American guards on the door; no one could enter without their credentials being closely scrutinised.

If my nyloned entry and my being a female, made any impression it was difficult to tell, for all the brass hats looked so severe, it was terrifying for me and must have been torture for the prisoner, who was standing to attention in the dock. He was a tall good-looking young man something like Clark Gable. I had no idea what he was charged with and I hoped I would be able to take shorthand fast enough or legibly enough to discover his crime, for by the looks on the faces of the prosecutors he must have been a heinous fellow.

At the other end of the room were double doors with a brass bar across each one, like the cinema doors which the attendants open with a clatter to let the audience out. There were no guards on this door and I assumed in a vague way that it was locked and guarded.

The Court was in session. I was called upon to swear under the flag. Now I could understand patriotism, for the sight of the Stars and Stripes sent a tingle down my spine. The Prosecutor began. One point on my pencil broke, it seemed like a pistol-shot in that solemn room. Grateful to my Sergeant, I turned my pencil round. I must be careful not to press so hard, I thought. I was not worried that I couldn't get the prisoner's army number down, I knew I'd be given that afterwards and I began to keep pace with the case. I was rather startled that they kept calling the prisoner A. Wall, for I was sure that wasn't his name in the beginning and they seemed to say his name in the strangest places that didn't make sense. The pace hotted up and I had forgotten everything except my shorthand, when suddenly there came a heavy crash at the end of the room. The 'cinema' doors opened with a mighty blow and in came 'Dirty Gertie' with the very latest in cleaning equipment, a monster vacuum-cleaner. She was a civilian employed by the British Government to clean parts of the hospital. She had been bombed out from London, her name was Gertie and I don't know where the 'Dirty' came from or indeed why this appellation was tacked on to her name, possibly because the words rhymed. She was a large, fat, peroxided woman who always wore the latest fashions, which looked incongruous on her. She had thick wedged-heel shoes which she seemed to have difficulty in lifting from the floor, and the dog-end of an American cigarette hanging from her mouth. The whole Court gazed at Gertie in a stupor. She ignored everyone as though we were invisible to her, and plugged in her new electric invention which made an unholy noise in that place of legal severity. The President of the Court recovered first and began shouting loudly at Gertie above the noise. Finally she realised her attention was being sought but without turning the cleaner off she mouthed, 'You'll have to shout, I can't hear you above this noise.' Finally one of the guards pulled the plug from the wall and the President said quite calmly, as though Gertie was an alien he had to placate, 'Can't you do that when the court rises?' Said Gertie laconically, 'Needs must when the devil drives!' and plugging in again, she resumed her conscientious cleaning. I was wondering what would happen when she reached us humans proper, I was sure she'd say, 'Mind out of my way! I have to work even if you lot have got nothing better to do than sit around staring at each other.' Perhaps she thought we were all rehearsing for a Camp concert. However, she was at last unplugged and marched off by the guards, her last remark being, 'Well, you can get your wives to soil their hands. I can't come back and clean this afternoon.'

The Court assumed its previous severity but I wondered if I imagined the wink from one of the brass hats. Possibly I did for I was now in a state of hysteria, trying to control my giggles.

The hut were convulsed when I acted out the case for them on my return. I completely forgot I had been sworn to secrecy and they were convinced that 'Towser' had stage-managed Gertie's entry. A few weeks later I saw the prisoner at a Saturday night dance. 'Oh, they didn't shoot you then,' I said. 'Gee, ma'am,' he said, 'For being absent without leave?' Of course, A. Wall was AWOL (absent without leave) and the poor dear had simply been tempted by a lady he met in Colchester.

CHAPTER NINE

The Prescription

We had marvellous lunches at the American hospital. No shortage of food there. Steaks, fruit etc., all beautifully cooked. The typists used to lunch in the officers' restaurant, although we had a table of our own. Music played, mostly classical, and Eileen, another girl there, taught me a lot about classical music so that I began to have a great appreciation for it. The first piece of music she 'explained' to me was Fingal's Cave, and ever after, although it sounded the same, it had a different meaning for me and I could follow the various changes of theme.

I had never been a large eater and now with all this rich food, which appeared richer because of our sparse rations, I suppose I should have tucked in and enjoyed my lunch-time as the other girls did. My thoughts, however, were on Marjorie and the children. What would they be having for lunch in the cottage in the village? How could I possibly eat and be merry? Then, too, the Americans had pineapple with their steaks. To me that was two meals, so I began to bring with me linen serviettes from home. I'd place my steak in one serviette and my fruit in another, and eat what was left on my plate, such as vegetables etc. The other girls thought this a good idea, but as there seemed so much food on the serving-tables they not only ate their portion but took extra to take home to their children. There was, too, on the top table, always a huge mound of oranges and the girls would casually take one as they left although really they were for diners who didn't want the dessert on the menu. However, as my father would have said, 'Someone always gets too greedy'—the kitchen staff were having to cook more and requisition for more because of the Mother Hubbards and so the lunches became chargeable instead of free and we had to be served individually from a hatch instead of helping ourselves. Of course the single girls then took a dim view of mother-love!

As a secretary to an American officer a jeep would call for me each morning and the driver would salute me when I opened the door at his knock. As Marjorie and I also had transport to and from hospital dances the local villagers, I am sure, thought we were fast 'Lunnon' women, especially as we had the army personnel home to tea. For one thing they were so generous with their food. They would come loaded up with things for the children, but we only ever invited the men and boys who were homesick for their mums and wives and children, whatever anyone else liked to suspect. We were lonely for our menfolk too and the visitors would play with the children and then when they were in bed play cards with us and have a really homely time. In any case Marjorie always saw the red light, if I may put it that way, before I did and the amorous ones were definitely not asked again.

My in-laws had moved down to a cottage not far from us so Susan still had grandparents who entertained her and Marjorie's ma-in-law and sister-in-law, both bombed out from London, lived next door, so we were a large happy family and hardly in a position to become Lilli Marlenes. One day we were walking home with two of my office colleagues who were coming to tea with us when we saw my lovely ma-in-law. She smiled and I waved and I said to my companion, 'That's my mother-in-law.' 'Jeeze,' he gulped, 'where I come from any ma-in-law would have dashed straight into the house and come out shooting.' 'But she knows me,' I said. 'That's as maybe,' he replied. 'But the mothers-in-law we have back home would have shot first and asked questions afterwards!' I thought he must have come from primitive territory.

Marjorie's small son Richard was now able to start school and through the influence of the Major she began to work in the PX store at the hospital. She could have had an exciting time socially because she was very attractive and there were so many American males dying to be 'comforted', but the brain-washing we had received from my mother from an early age as to the way 'decent' women conduct their lives, had made Marjorie as nun-like as I tried to be. What with working all day, looking after the children, the household chores, and writing to Chas at night, I had neither the inclination nor the energy to cope with an amorous interlude, but I often wondered, whether, had I lived on my own during the war, I would have refused all the wonderful 'opportunities' which endlessly presented themselves.

In one way I suppose Marjorie kept me on the straight and narrow. One sergeant in my office received a fabulous cake from home, I think it was a Simnel cake. It was covered with cherries, marzipan, nuts, and angelica. The sight of it was enough to take one's breath away in those days of austerity. The Sergeant said, 'That's for you, Dorothy, if I can have a cup of coffee with you one day.' 'Indeed, you'd be very welcome any time,' I said delightedly. I took the cake home and watched the children's faces. The cake was as marvellous inside as it was out. I have never tasted anything like it and Marjorie said, 'What a generous man he must be, Dolly.'

At ten p.m. the next night came a thunderous banging on the cottage door. We had no bell or knocker. Before the war and before the 'foreigners' invaded the village no one seemed to lock their doors. I popped my head out of the bedroom window. There was the Simnel-cake sergeant and he was shouting, 'I've come for my cup of coffee, Towser.' I was absolutely terrified. What would the neighbours think? 'Hush,' I called down in a hoarse whisper, 'You'll wake the children up.' Still he wouldn't go but kept calling, 'Towser, Towser, you promised me.' Finally Marjorie called down to him, 'If you don't go away we'll call the police.' In the end he went off into the darkness and I heard him say, 'Bloody dames, they're all the same, lead you on, take all you've got and give you nothing.' We lay in bed in the darkness. I was full of remorse that we had eaten the cake, but Marjorie felt me very stupid not to have realised 'what sort of man' the Sergeant was, which annoyed me and didn't help my ego. Surely I was worth more than a Simnel cake?

The next day as I passed the Sergeant's desk he gave me a look so malevolent that I said, 'I'm very sorry but you did call rather late at night for coffee, especially in a small country village.' 'You led me on,' he shouted so viciously, that in front of the listening G.I.s, all agog at the Sergeant's frustrated rage, I felt not only nervous but acutely embarrassed. 'When I gave you the cake,' he went on chokingly, 'you said, *any time* it would be *your pleasure.*' So he had been deceived by my polite expression. I went hot under the collar, then I became very angry and I said distantly, 'Well I am very sorry that we have eaten your lovely cake and I am more than sorry we have been talking at cross purposes. I assumed that because of your yearning for coffee so late at night you were some sort of coffee addict.' This seemed to cause great amusement to the rest of the hut and for weeks afterwards one or other of the G.I.s would make some casual remark about coffee. They'd say, 'Oh, gee, I had a smashing cup of coffee last night,' or they'd bring me a box of tea-bags and say, 'Towser doesn't like coffee' or 'You know, Towser, if you once tasted coffee the American way, you'd love it;' but of course, never when the Simnel cake sergeant was present for he never got over the shock of its loss.

Possibly my father was one of the 'foreigners' who taught the locals to lock their doors. We had persuaded my parents to come away from the bombing and Mother was so thrilled to be with us again. Our cottage was in a row of identical unnumbered residences. One night my father had been to the local pub. It was pitch black when he came home and he fell into the cottage next door, saying, 'God, it's bloody dark! Have you gone to bed already, Mother? Never mind I'll find my way up.' Unfortunately in the cottage next door lived an ancient lady, and she was sitting by her fire in the dark when my father burst in. Her screams and yells alerted the neighbours and my father was more terrified than she was for she was mumbling all sorts of terrible things about him. Ever after when she saw him she would point and yell, 'That's him, bor, that's him.'

It would have been the easiest thing in the world for me to remain, for the whole duration of the war, in my blessed state of chastity—no belt needed where Dolly was concerned—for in my teen-age years, my twenties, and now my thirties, few male heads turned at my approach or passing. For the sake of Marjorie and various girl-friends, unable to attend dances unaccompanied, I had sat for hours on various types of uncomfortable chairs, little gilt affairs, wooden kitchen chairs, and benches. I achieved over the years that pride-saving air of nonchalant aloofness. Indeed the very role of wallflower caused me to take up smoking, for something to occupy my hands, which are ever the most awkward parts of a wallflower's make-up. I sometimes cursed the waste of time, but it would have been tempting providence to take knitting or crochet to a dance. Who knows, there might be one male who saw a lusting luscious siren curled up inside my façade of motherliness?

I had never been without male companionship before marriage, but mainly because Marjorie and friends, always inundated with invitations to dance, brought their partners back to introduce them to me and make a social group for the evening. By a bit of sharp repartee I often gained a male companion but lost a girl-friend. I doubt if my husband would now admit it, but at the time of our meeting he was enamoured of a beautiful creature.

I always had a way with children, and they never failed to gravitate towards me, so perhaps it was the small boy in most men which finally made them admirers. But it was all so unsatisfactory and I longed for that startled look of joy from a man when he first set eyes on me. However it was too late in life for me to expect love at first sight so it was quite easy to live the life of a nun whilst Chas was away. I was safe by nature! When the matrons of the village gossiped about the 'goings on' between 'women who should know better' and the British Tommy, or American G.I., I remained silent. I would have been a hypocrite to join in the castigation, for I was not sure at that time that I would have been quite so upright should the right G.I. affirm his intentions. It would have been difficult to break loose living as I did with Marjorie, always the noblest Roman of them all, and with Chas's relations surrounding us.

One day I was taking the children blackberrying when I met an old schoolfriend. Her husband, too, was in the forces abroad, she had been bombed out from London and was staying in a cottage in a nearby village. Her children, two boys, were older than my daughter and they had cycled over to our village for a picnic. The years forgotten, we chatted excitedly and she persuaded me to come the following Saturday to the weekly dance which was held at the nearby American airfield. She would ask the driver of the transport vehicle to come through our village and pick me up and then bring me home at the end of the evening. She assured me I would 'have the time of my life', for she added, 'You were always such a lad, Dolly Chegwidden.' I was surprised at her description of me, for in my memory I was always intensely serious and proper at school.

Marjorie said she would baby-sit for me, and I began to prepare excitedly for this grand occasion. The great day came and I waited like a bird of paradise in my unusual plumage. I had raked out a forgotten evening dress, ankle-length, sleeveless, low-necked black velvet, which I had been steaming all the afternoon, making the kitchen like a Turkish bath. Fortunately Marjorie had gone visiting and I just had time to dry the windows and open the doors before she arrived home. I had dyed some white satin shoes black, they were still a bit smelly with the strong dye, and Marjorie sniffed distastefully, but this didn't really perturb me for she always has gone around smelling smells other people are unaware of. My elbow-length gloves were pristinely white and Marjorie, in a moment of sisterly love, fetched her little gold stole for me.

The children were asleep when the 'transport' came. My first shock. It was the largest lorry I had ever seen, simply enormous. It had stopped outside our cottage and the driver, in American uniform, knocked on our cottage door. There was no time to draw back now, and the object of curious eyes, it seemed to me all the lace-curtains in the village were twitching, I followed the driver to the back of the lorry. There, to my utter horror, was a very long ladder for me to climb. Another G.I. was in the lorry at the top of the ladder and I negotiated these rungs and climbed into the darkness with his help. The vehicle was crammed full with giggling, screaming girls, but the noise ceased at my entry as though someone had turned off a switch. Here was Dame Nellie Melba in person. All the other girls were clad informally. Little cotton frocks or jumpers and skirts, flat-heeled or wedge-soled shoes. There was no sign of my friend. What a fool I had been, I felt like a prize cow amongst a herd of cattle. I thought perhaps I could find a place at the dance where I could hide myself until the lorry returned later that night. I might even be able to get transport home right away. I was furious that I hadn't made some excuse when the lorry called, but it had been so high that I couldn't see the type of load it was transporting.

We arrived at the air-base, an enormous place with rows and rows of barracks, but no sign of planes; I supposed they were in another part of the 'drome. Like a guard of honour lined up, we were met by happy smiling servicemen, and most of the girls were soon pounced on and led off to the dance floor. I could hear the strains of music in the distance, and never never had I seen so many men before. The driver called out, 'Leaving at midnight, ladies,' and drove away. I was left alone. I had five hours to wait. I have never had any sense of direction and I thought I should be afraid to leave the spot where the lorry had left us for I might have been unable to find it again in the dark. I realised suddenly that the girls on the lorry had assumed I was an 'entertainer' for they used to have visiting singers and such like at the camp dances.

Suddenly from among a nearby group of airmen I heard one say, 'O.K. then, I'll take the Duchess,' and a tall good-looking serviceman approached me and said, 'Take my arm then, Duchess.' He had obviously been drinking and so had his companions. 'I'm waiting for the Duke,' I replied, and trying to take a quick note of my bearings I walked in the direction of the music. The dance was held in a sort of hangar. It was a mass of jigging couples, not dancing at all in the way Marjorie and I had been used to. I found a seat and sat down in a corner, willing the next five hours to fly. An air-force sergeant came up and I went on to the 'floor' with him. Cheek to alcoholic cheek we 'danced', me struggling with Marjorie's stole, my evening bag, and his hands, which seemed to be so tired they could only rest on my bottom. At last the music stopped. The sergeant looked at me, gazed at my outfit, and said, 'Gee, you're a real classy dame, I bet you don't come from these parts.' 'No,' I said, pleased that the dance had stopped, 'I come from London.' He looked as though he'd been presented with the Purple Heart for he said delightedly, 'Anywhere near Piccadilly or Ly-cest-er Square?' 'Oh, no,' I said, wondering why he had picked on that area. 'Come and have something to drink,' he said. Pleased not to be asked to dance again I went with him to the refreshment room. He seemed disappointed I only wanted Coke but he looked nicer now he was off the dance floor, and as he also had a Coke I began to think I was mistaken in thinking he had been drinking, for he began to speak so sensibly. He was a Texan, married, very happily, it seemed and he had two children. I began to relax; the next few hours would pass safely in the company of this happily married man, and I would never have to come to a camp dance again.

It was dark now, but the weather humid, and when Carl, for that was his name, invited me for a walk to cool off before we resumed dancing, I agreed. Heads did turn as we walked through the hall, for Carl was one of those tall, well-built Texans, and he had that sinuous easy glide such Texans have. It is true I am short, but all done up in velvet and mock diamonds, we were certainly an outstanding pair.

We walked round the camp, Carl put my arm in his, and all was quite pleasant, minutes ticking away easily for me, until we rounded a tall hedge bordering the lawn of a garden. Suddenly Carl's arm went round me and he began to bite my neck. He didn't expect my kick on his shin and as he reeled back I kicked off my high-heeled shoes and began to run like mad towards the lights of the camp. When I was nearing the safety of the dance hall I looked back and saw my Texan walking quickly in my direction. A jeep was outside the dance-hall, the driver just getting in. I said to him breathlessly, 'Is it possible you can give me a lift, I've just had an urgent message from home.' Whether it was my phantom-of-the-opera-like appearance or the hint of tragedy in my urgent message I don't know, for Army and Air Force personnel do not give lifts to anyone, especially civilians, without chitties or some official permit, but to my delight he agreed, and I arrived back to the blessed haven of our cottage. My missing shoes puzzled Marjorie for a long, long time. I should have realised a casual 'Oh, I forgot I had them on,' would not be an acceptable explanation to her.

The dances at the American hospital were very different and pleasant social evenings. The G.I.s had an old-fashioned courtesy and charming manners. Our special group were young men from the laboratory, only one of them, Felix, was married. Marjorie taught them the English ballroom dancing and we had pleasant if uninspired Saturdays. Until the Saturday Felix suggested we take a turn round the grounds between dances. There was no worry of neck-biting or anything untoward with Felix, he was a typical specimen of clean-living American manhood, the sort of fellow I would one day like for a son. Suddenly he said, 'I saw the M.O. today.' 'Oh, I am sorry, Felix,' I said. 'Anything serious?' 'Oh, no,' he said, 'Nothing medically wrong, it's just that when a man has been married and is then separated from his wife for a long time, it can affect his health.' I was silent, embarrassment beginning to creep over me; how stupid I am, I thought, Felix obviously wants to talk to me as a mother-figure. 'There is no solution, though, is there, Felix?' I said. 'Well,' said Felix, 'there is. The Doctor knows you very well and he knows you too are separated from your husband, and that the separation will be a long one. He knows, too, that you are a clean-living girl and he thought it would be a good idea, not hurting anyone, for we both love our partners, if you and I could form some sort of association, and be faithful to each other. In that way, we'd be happy, and not be hurting anyone else.'

I was silent, seething because the Doctor's diagnosis was, to me, a real insult. He was a real dish and lately had been making special trips to the office, or on Saturdays at the dances, to chat with me. I thought he had 'fallen' for me and I was toying with the thought in my mind, would I, should I, if he approached me. So that's why he had been gazing at me, summing me up as a sort of pill, a tonic, a prescription for one of his patients. Then I looked at Felix, he was looking so pleadingly at me that although I felt cross with him I also felt sorry for him; perhaps it was worse for a man than a woman. But as for the other matter, good God, I was his friend, his confidante, I felt old enough to be his mother, why I was ten years, no, six years older than he. 'Well, Felix,' I said, 'I am sorry that if you love your wife you cannot be strong-willed enough to be faithful to her. I could never ever be unfaithful to my husband, for any man.' I kept my fingers crossed as these words of near-mendacity issued from my lips. 'Please don't stop being friends with me, Towser,' said Felix. 'I knew you would say no, but the Doctor said approach the matter from a humanist point of view.' I had no idea there was such a word as 'humanist' and I assumed it should have been 'humane'.

On Monday morning the Doctor came into the office. The Major was not there. 'Did you see Felix at the dance on Saturday?' he asked, adding, 'I saw him across the parade-ground, but he kept on walking.' 'Oh, like his namesake,' I said, still typing. This feeble joke was obviously lost on him for he suddenly jumped back from me, startled. 'Do you feel all right?' he asked. 'Yes, of course I do,' I replied. 'Well, I don't want to worry you, my dear, but you look jaundiced, to me.' 'Jaundiced!' I screamed, thinking he was crazy, but as he was a good medical man, I was a little perturbed. 'Look here,' he said, 'I'll give you a pass, go to the laboratory and have a check-up, it'll only take a minute.' He put a form on my desk and left the room hurriedly for he saw my Major approaching. 'What did *he* want again?' asked the Major. 'He says I'm jaundiced,' I said, 'and he suggests I have a test at the lab.' 'Come here, Towser,' he said, walking to the window. 'Well,' he said, after gazing closely at my face, 'I can't see any change in you.' Then he added, 'You've got those tawny sort of eyes and freckles, they go with your colour of hair. Why is he so interested in you all of a sudden?' I was much too shy with the Major to tell him that the Doctor wished to make a prescription of me. Soon the whole hut was in examining 'Towser' and all came to the same conclusion, the Doctor was wrong. But I went to the laboratory just to prove he was wrong. The boys there too were interested, Eddie, Bill and Gerry, our Saturday-night friends. The test was O.K. I was not jaundiced, well not medically or physically so, but temperamentally I was extremely jaundiced with the Doctor.

In the week he invited me to dinner and the theatre, and I thought this would be the opportunity for me to 'have it out with him'. I knew I looked nice when I met him and we had a marvellous evening, with drinks after the theatre, so that, more relaxed, I took up the matter of Felix. He *had* told Felix what Felix had told me, but was indignant that Felix should have chosen me for his physick. He hadn't even mentioned my name, indeed he would not; why, he wanted me for himself. I could see this was true, and indeed he was an attractive man. The night was balmy, and so must I have been, for I was sure I would end up in some grassy buttercupped meadow by the side of a scented hedge. It was three miles from the theatre to my cottage, we started walking. With my companion's arm round my waist, my head on his shoulder, we fitted perfectly, and walked happily to what might just prove to be our mutual resting-place.

Suddenly, just as we had decided to turn off from the road, an American Staff car stopped. The driver got out, saluted smartly, and said, 'May I give you a lift back to Camp, Sir?' In the back of the car was my Major. He opened the door and said, 'We can drop Towser first.' There was nothing for it, the Major was like a watch-dog. The Doctor could not blemish my reputation by saying he wouldn't be going straight back to Camp and he knew that the Major knew that I lived in the village with Marjorie and the children. Obviously that was where I *had* seemed to be going and the car would save me a walk.

I got in the car as the Doctor said under his breath, 'Dammit, I could spit.' The Major asked, 'Was the play good?' I started to laugh, which started the Major and the driver off, but not the Doctor. He remained silent. Next day he was transferred and was sent to Italy.

The G.I.s were always cheerful and there was much teasing and friendly rivalry between us as to the merits of our respective armies. The Americans thought our press very strange in its reports of the war. I was greeted one day with, 'Towser, you're doing well, your Monty's a marvel. Do you know he's actually gained an "inch" of territory from the Germans today?' The headline splashed across the paper, read, 'Monty's troops inch forward.' They brought a foot ruler to impress on me how well Monty was doing.

But of course I had my own back. One of my duties was the typing of the payroll for the incoming wounded. Always a rush job and sometimes I would stay late in the evening to complete it. On the pay parade-morning the walking wounded would come in in ones or twos, in dressing-gowns, or perhaps just pyjamas, casually collect their money from the Major, and saunter out. After a most bloody battle in Germany, a train-load of British wounded were temporarily accommodated over-night at the American hospital and the Major and I worked late on the payroll for the Tommies. Next morning in came the English wounded and I could hardly stem my tears. Many of the men were badly wounded, yet their clothes were tidy, there was no slouching and they all managed a salute—a most disciplined and military payroll parade. All was quiet in the Nissen hut after the last Tommy had left. But the next payroll day the poor wounded G.Is. must have wondered what had hit them for Milton J. had them 'marched' in with a sergeant and they all saluted. As the last American left Milton J. looked at me and said, 'Maa,' just as we did when we were children and of course we both laughed. 'I didn't know it showed,' I said. But we both knew it wasn't the saluting or the spit and polish which counted, for one could not but admire the Americans' spirit and buoyancy and I never ceased to be amazed at their talent for efficient organisation. The whole camp ran on oiled wheels without the superfluous intrusion of bureaucracy or red tape. They were kind and generous people (and I'm not thinking of the Simnel-cake episode) and extremely outgoing.

Chas was now out of North Africa and we had been apart for nearly three years. He tried to be amusing in his letters, but a serious man by nature, I know he was trying to make the best of things. Always a bad sailor, he would have been sea-sick in a rowing-boat on glass; the journey away from England must have been sheer torture. Loaded to capacity with British and American soldiers, the diet was stew, or as one G.I. remarked, 'Bloody boiled sheep again.' The Americans would shoot crap, or play cards, and in the enclosed conditions knife-fights often took place. Chas said no one was ever hurt, it was just a show of strength. Nerves were frayed to breaking-point. To get to meals or even to the lavatory, meant hours of endless queuing. Then something went wrong with the steering and they couldn't keep up with the convoy, a sitting-duck for a German submarine. Chas was working night and day in North Africa and Italy. At least he had air to breathe. He was in charge of troop-movement schedules and many famous names passed through the R.A.T.D. Depot, among them Harry Secombe. I think he was 'resting' after having been wounded. He was very popular, always a fine chap, and used to entertain the men with farmyard imitations, 'Here comes Farmer Brown with his dog . . .' I suppose with a passing population his act was always fresh!

Since he received his black eye on initial training Chas had always been a unit clerk and not called upon to bear arms or shoot, but at one time it was 'everybody out', for German parachutists were landing in a nearby corn-field where the corn really was 'as high as an elephant's eye'. Chas said he was very relieved not to meet a German parachutist in the corn-field. Word went round that the Germans were disguised as nuns! I wondered, if Chas would be quick enough to gain the initiative, or if he would give a 'nun' too much time to prove that she was a lady, for I couldn't imagine him shooting in cold blood.

Chas had a fine officer, a Captain Derek Attwood, a wonderful cricketer and footballer, from Bromley in Kent, my father's old stamping-ground. This officer nearly lost his life swimming miles out to sea to rescue one of his men who had got into difficulties. The sea was so rough that the boat the men tried to launch capsized and was tossed up and down like a cockleshell. He ordered all his men to stay on the shore and dragging the boat he swam out to sea, somehow got the man in the boat and swam back with it. He was all-in, and the man he rescued was black with having been in the water so long. It was a miracle they both recovered. But to Chas's amazement after this life-and-death struggle with the elements the Captain still emerged wearing his peaked cap and with his gun still in its holster.

The men would long for and wait anxiously for the water-waggon when they were stationed in the desert. When the mobile bath unit arrived, a huge marquee would be set up, its monster of an engine coughing and spluttering. The men would undress, leave their clothes in a heap and then march through the shower. The marquee echoed with the shouts, yells, tortured screams and the cries of the men, for the engine would cough freezing water and boiling water alternately, but never the right temperature of water, so that although the shower was a longed-for 'must' it was also a time to be dreaded. When they tottered from the marquee they were handed freshly laundered clothes. It was a lucky dip, to say the least of it, for the bundles were not separated as to size, or condition of the garments. A large soldier would be handed the underclothes of a dwarf, or vice versa. A soldier who had conscientiously mended his clothes and darned his socks could be handed socks with great 'potatoes' in them and garments with the buttons hanging off. There was much swopping and changing after the bath, but no one would part with any item in a good condition if it could possibly be made to fit so the conscientious ones were always very indignant after bath-time, feeling very hard done by if they saw a careless compatriot lording it about in what they suspected were their good socks.

Sometimes, whilst troops were on the move, letters home were delayed. At one time as I had not heard from Chas for weeks and weeks, and as he always wrote regularly, I wondered whether I should write to the War Office. Before my father beat his hurried retreat to Forest Gate I asked his advice about this. Soldiering being a part of his life, he would be 'in the know'. He decided I was being a weak little woman and would waste the time of the War Office with my enquiry. 'Let 'em get on with the job they're doing,' was his attitude. My letter would not bring my darling back 'if he'd gone'. Then one day I received a parcel from abroad. Great excitement in the family, 'Open it quickly, Dolly, it's a present from Chas.' The label was printed, but we assumed it was from him. I took off the wrapping to reveal an urn-shaped tin and on opening this was startled and mystified to find it contained an amount of dark ashy metallic-like powder. 'Whatever could it be?' My father sniffed it, then took a pinch between his fingers, then to our horror, lightly licked it. As he spat it out, he said darkly, 'Something's got dehydrated here.' Because I had a sick feeling about this dark powdery substance I was loth to dispose of it, but at my father's insistence, 'You never know what the children might catch,' I washed it down the drain. I warned the family not to mention the parcel to my ma-in-law, for she was frantic at not having heard from Chas for so long.

This wretched ash was in my dreams with me, until the day I received a letter from Chas. Under separate cover he had sent some of the 'dust' from Vesuvius. The volcano had erupted, covering their tent and even breaking the tent-poles. He said it was an unnerving experience and he would tell me all about it on his return. It had been an unnerving experience for me too, but I could hardly tell him why.

CHAPTER TEN

Loving Couples

The one thing which really bothered me about life in rural England was the primitive outdoor sanitation. When the men came to 'collect' in the dead of night, I wondered what fate had decreed that they should follow this depressing way of life. Only a huge remuneration could have recompensed them, yet it was probably 'the poorer the job the poorer the pay' and I never knew the identity of these men. Dark shadowy figures, muffled thumping, eerie sucking and gurgling noises from their giant soup-ladles, these were the Night Soil Men.

The cottages to the left of us had their own fenced-off gardens, but we shared a 'privy' with another cottage which adjoined a side lane, therefore we had no garden but a large dirt area at the bottom of which was the sanitary building. Between the cottages was an alleyway so that our convenience could be approached by the public, which added to its inconvenience. We had to watch little Richard for he took great joy in throwing things down the rough hewn hole in the wooden seat in the privy platform and neither Marjorie nor I would have been brave enough to rescue anything, however precious. The people with whom we shared our 'mod. cons' had a large number of evacuees with them from time to time and at night in the pitch darkness one could observe waving lanterns, like giant glow-worms, in the vicinity of the privy. Marjorie and I, however, disciplined ourselves and only visited this outside building during the hours of daylight, the whole family making a hurried last visit before the country night fell with its velvet blackness and untownlike sounds.

The cottage stairs wound round the cottage like a jointed arm, and at the bottom possessed a door with a Suffolk latch, leading directly into the kitchen and a door at the top with the same Suffolk latch leading to the bedrooms, so these narrow dangerous stairs were self-contained when both doors were closed. On the bend of the stairs at night-time we would place a white enamel pail for emergencies for neither Marjorie nor I would face the terrors we were sure would roam by night, and cross the dark yard. These stairs were over the coal-hole and water running into the pail made weird sounding noises in the quiet little cottage, the hollow coal cellar carrying the sound, but as Marjorie and I were the only listeners we suffered no embarrassment, that is, of course, until the evening of the Vicar's visit.

He did not call on a routine visit to his parishioners for our visits to church were rare, we were so busy. He had recently come to the village from Australia, where he and his wife, an officer in the Wrens, had met our older sister Winifred. They had become friends with her, being on the same *social* scale down under and were on first-name terms. Winifred's grammar-school education had given her a higher-class social status than Marjorie and I aspired to. Just after she and Sydney were married they'd emigrated to Australia. Winifred said that sometimes on their farm in the Australian bush she almost heard the grass growing, so homesick did she become for the sounds of London. They had a ram on the farm which Winnie had nicknamed 'Sam'. A friendly name, I felt, for what was obviously such a vicious creature. I had no idea that a sheep could be so wicked. This Sam was an enormous beast with vicious horns. It was his aim in life to 'get' a human. It was their aim he should not.

Winnie was one day in a very narrow passageway between animal pens, singing away, unaware that Sydney had let Sam out of his pen at the other end of the passageway behind her. Whether Syd was in a temper with Win for some reason or other, or whether he was just being absent-minded, I don't know, but this ram came tearing along the passageway like a mad bull, the dream of his little sheepy life was to be realised. As he gathered momentum a shout of 'Look out, missus, it's Sam,' came from the old bush man, who adored the 'missus', and Winnie, because she was so agile, just managed to leap in with some cows in the nick of time.

To hear Winnie talk later one would assume that W.A., as she called Western Australia, was the best place on earth, paradise in fact. Yet they toiled for years to obtain a bumper wheat harvest and then when they did there was a wheat slump and wheat was dumped into the sea. Then Syd was taken suddenly ill. Winnie was at that time alone on the farm with him. She got out the horse and waggon and drove him many miles to the railway-siding to send him to hospital. She returned to the farm, lost her way in the bush, and the wretched horse would not budge. She didn't like the idea of spending the night in the bush without protection (I would have died instantly) so she let the horse have its head and he turned round and found his own way home! But when she arrived, disaster had struck again. Her house was burnt to the ground. She waited until morning, then went to Perth and obtained a job working for the Archbishop there until her husband left hospital. It was while she was working for the Archbishop that she'd met our vicar.

I was occupying our emergency 'loo' when the vicar entered our cottage. Startled by the mysterious 'noises off' which he obviously took to be whirring and crunching sounds on the gravel road, he enquired of Marjorie in his bright clergyman's tone of voice, 'Someone enjoying an evening's bicycling?' 'Yes,' replied Marjorie, acutely embarrassed, 'my sister Dorothy.' Unaware of all this I entered the room and said, 'Oh, good evening, Vicar.' 'I hope you enjoyed your bicycling in the dark?' he enquired of me, with warm interest. 'Bicycling?' I queried, having difficulty in pronouncing the word in my best speech, Marjorie's gestures and contortions failing utterly to put me in the picture. 'I have never been able to ride a bicycle, although I would very much like to learn.' Sadly I added, 'I've never possessed one.'

Marjorie quickly offered the vicar some tea, but with a strange look at us both he departed, saying it was only a flying visit just to tell us all about dear Winifred, a great friend of theirs. He hoped he'd see us in church and the safety of our husbands would be requested in his prayers. He left very quickly. As the door closed Marjorie exploded and then said to me, 'Oh, Dee, you really must be more careful.'

Care was a difficult, if not impossible thing to exercise, for the cottages were only made of lath and plaster. We always knew what Fred next door was up to. He was in the Home Guard and in the privacy of his bedroom not only cleaned his rifle, but also drilled with it. We often heard his tired wife call plaintively, 'Fred, do stop playing with your gun, bor,' which always brought an infuriated shout from Fred for he knew how important was the Home Guard. In any case Fred always made it plain to his wife that he was not 'playing' with his gun, which indeed, according to Fred, 'was not a bloody gun, mor, but a rifle,' but his wife was always insulting his wand of office.

However, the Vicar's untimely query had aroused in me again my lifelong desire to learn to ride a bicycle. Nancy, Charlie's young cousin, very generously offered me the loan of her bicycle and Marjorie and her friend Pat decided to teach me. They had ridden bicycles all their lives, to them it was a simple matter and they insisted it would take only a short time to make me proficient. But of course I was over thirty, awkward and extremely nervous of this two-wheeled machine and the country lanes were now busy with wartime traffic—army lorries, jeeps and great oil-tankers which tore non-stop through the country villages. I was the only member of the Chegwidden family unable to ride a bicycle, with the exception of my parents, of course. I could never visualise my mother on a penny-farthing, and my father hated everything on two wheels. 'I'll stick to Shank's pony,' he would say, forgetting that all his life he had said to us, 'We must move with the times.' He had never got over the time when he had been browbeaten into taking a ride in my brother Arthur's car. It was the first car in the family, indeed the only one amongst all our friends, neighbours and acquaintances. It had cost Arthur, second-hand, £5. It was a huge vehicle open to the elements. Arthur had taken Father for just a little ride round the streets, Father becoming increasingly terrified at Arthur's chatting away to him. Sitting solitarily in the back seat, which was like a long plank, he was entreating Arthur not to talk when the back seat collapsed and a sprawling Father screamed from the floor, 'Don't turn round, I'm all right, just you keep your eyes on the bloody road.' Father came home tottery and swearing while Arthur arrived back in hysterics.

The first hour of my lesson was excruciatingly painful, taking place in a somewhat dangerous spot, down a lane, beside which ran a river leading to a weir. Pat and Marjorie were in hysterics when I ran off the road, up a steep incline of a bank to the hedge, and returned more quickly backwards still seated. I was sure that the mighty bump I sustained on reaching the level of the lane again would alter not only my future stance, but possibly even my future behaviour. When I hovered perilously near the weir they suggested finding a safer training-ground, and advised that on the way to this safe area I should cycle along the main road of the village to 'give me confidence'. I commenced without too much wobbling, but the girls had forgotten the evening petrol-tankers on their furious journey to the Air Force Base. 'Don't look at them,' screamed Marjorie, for it appeared the tankers were mesmerising me. 'Turn right!' yelled Pat when we came to a narrow turning. I was, of course, 'leading the way', my teachers were there merely to pick up the pieces. I wobbled 'right', up a slope off the main road and without seeming volition on my part, then turned left. I now found myself in an extremely dark lane, very narrow, on the right of which was another river, or was it the same one which I had come to escape from, winding itself about and following my progress like a monstrous snake. On the left was the back of a dark satanic mill and hanging from the wall were the wheels and tackle which hoisted the sacks of flour up and down from a pit beneath.

The roadway adjoining the mill at this spot was extremely narrow, therefore very dangerous for me to negotiate as I could so easily cycle down the bank into the river on the right, but at this spot, although the river was unfenced, it had widened out and was on the shallow side. Now yells from Pat and Marjorie for me to be careful, to look straight ahead, to brake, for they saw simultaneously, a different sort of hazard which faced me on the narrow roadway. By my unguided wobbling into unexplored places I had brought the three of us into a situation beyond our ken. On the narrow roadway in front of me were three motionless people, not in the formation of a chatting group, or even three abreast. The group comprised two American airmen and a woman. The first man was facing the woman and she had her back to the front of the other man. Both had their arms tight round her.

As if in a dream they turned their heads to face me as I rode slowly and relentlessly towards them. They could have had no idea I was not in command of my vehicle, or even my senses, at that point. They may have expected me to stop, beg their pardon, turn round and ride away into the night with my companions, pretending I had seen nothing, for they seemed to 'close ranks' if that were possible. Suddenly from the depths of my subconscious I realised I had come unwittingly upon some tableau of 'love', and as if to escape automatically, I pressed harder on my pedals, unfortunately increasing my forward momentum. The glazed look on the face of the 'serviceman' on the right, turned to horror. 'Jesus, for crissake,' he screamed, and leapt backwards into the millstream, and as I flew through the centre of this unholy trinity, the remaining two participants, still locked in each other's arms, staggered forward and tumbled into the flour-pit.

I shot on at speed (suddenly an efficient cyclist) over a white-fenced bridge, through a field and into a haystack where I fell off the bicycle, bruised, shaken and breathless. A panting Marjorie and Pat soon caught me up and Marjorie conducted a hurried conclave. 'Do you think we should tell the police what we have seen?' she asked. Pat and I looked blankly at Marjorie. 'Suppose a little Brownie should come round the corner?' she continued. What had fairies to do with it? We looked more stupid at Marjorie's continued questions, and impatiently she explained it was the night for the Brownies and Guides to meet, and some of them walked home past the Old Mill. 'What we have seen,' said Marjorie dramatically, really not knowing what we had witnessed, I knew, 'would not be suitable for a Brownie.' 'Nor even a Brown Owl,' I added. 'It's no laughing matter, Dee,' complained Marjorie. 'Well,' I said, 'we've come to no harm and we have accidentally punished the unrighteous. What on earth would you say to the village sergeant, especially as those three are dusting and drying themselves off somewhere far away from here?'

We wheeled our bicycles home, Marjorie a little disapproving because I was amused at the thought of the village sergeant taking down, in his broad Suffolk accent, her statement of 'love in the raw'.

My parents-in-law had been baby-sitting for us and when my father-in-law asked how I had got on, I said, 'I may have performed the first ever circumcision by bicycle.' 'What a disgusting thing to say,' said Marjorie, and I whispered to Alfred that I'd tell him all about our two-wheeled adventure later. He had such a sense of humour and I often popped in to tell him anything amusing for life was a little quiet for him in the country, and as his eye-sight was failing he could hardly see to read the paper or a magazine. I knew he'd be in hysterics listening to the story of my ride.

But my pa-in-law was not destined to hear this tale of rustic passion for now it seemed that we were winning the war I decided it could manage very nicely without me. We would go back to London, Susan and I and prepare our home for one returning hero.

I could have had a ceremonious good-bye with my friends at the hospital, a party, exchanges of addresses, 'Don't forget, Towser, if you're ever in the little old U.S. of A,' sort of thing, but I remembered an expression of my father's regarding such occasions, 'Don't prolong the agony,' and I agreed with his unsentimental attitude to good-byes. It took the sting out of nostalgia. But I did have a farewell lunch with Maudie.

'My trouble,' said Maudie, analytically and unemotionally, 'My trouble has always been that I am unable to say "no", not because I don't want to say "no", but because, when I was a kid I was taught to say "yes" all the time. "It's rude to refuse, it's bad-mannered to say 'no'," they'd say, and now I just don't know how to. With my whisky distributor,' she said mysteriously, 'I didn't want to. I didn't like it, yet it was all because I didn't like to say "no", and look at the trouble it could have led to. I wonder,' went on Maudie, miles away in a philosophical pastureland of unreality, 'what a judge in a court would say if you said, "I just didn't like to refuse." It's the same with other things, and I've had another lucky escape there. Did I ever tell you about Ellen?'

Ellen, apparently, was an ex-colleague of Maudie's. She had come down to the country with her three small boys. A lovely-looking girl, she was good-natured and easy-going. She had been married quite young having been 'seduced' at a party when both she and a fellow guest were in that dangerous state of not being drunk exactly, but in that beautiful limbo land between, where everything is just that bit rosier than reality. Her chap had 'done the right thing by her' and married her, but they were totally unsuited and very unhappy. Maudie met Ellen at a war-time factory in Colchester where Ellen had met the man of her dreams, a young G.I., of comfortable parents, single and handsome. They were madly in love and wished to get married. Ellen told Maudie her divorce was through and Maudie was a witness at Ellen's wedding, blessed by permission of the American authorities. They left for the U.S. immediately after the wedding, where the bridegroom was to take up an important military post. Maudie said she thought everything was in order, why it *had* to be, the authorities were very careful of their young men away from home.

Maudie had signed all sorts of forms and affidavits for the two lovers and was shocked and worried when she discovered (after the wedding) that the decree nisi wasn't nicely 'nisi', but 'pending'. 'I always read what I sign now,' said Maudie, 'and I would advise you to do the same, Dolly.' 'What happened to Ellen in the end, did you ever hear?' 'Yes,' said Maudie, 'I had some marvellous photos from them after the war when everything *was* in order, and they sent me a gold locket as a thank-you present. They are still as happy, and have twin daughters, now, her home looks like a Spanish hacienda, her in-laws think the world of her, and she had another "wedding" in a cathedral out there. Every time I look at the locket though,' went on Maudie, 'I can see myself carted off to prison, it doesn't really do to trust even your best friend.'

Maudie herself took a down-to-earth view of life. Before the war she had been a normal wife and mother, happy in her marriage, loved and loving. I thought her honest because she had no furtive, prim, or narrow attitudes towards sharing her bed, and openly admitted she needed a 'sleeping' partner to keep her a happy and contented mother to her two children. I knew that after the war if her husband returned they would resume a contented married life, the past would probably never arise, for Maudie always 'kept her head'. There would be no surprise offspring to greet her demobbed husband, and each resident knew that she was waiting for her husband. What she offered them was a temporary haven and I believe she made life bearable for the pilots on their dangerous nightly missions over enemy territory.

She was kind and generous, helpful to those in trouble and had a great sense of humour. She told me of her first hilarious adventure into the realms of 'unfaithfulness'. She had been working for some months for a scientific and technical officer, a very serious man who checked and counter-checked facts and figures and who performed all his duties 'according to plan' never deviating from the printed instructions, leaving nothing to chance. He was a tall man with a fine physique, and Maudie said all the girls in her department were crazy about him because in addition to his god-like appearance he was aloof therefore appearing 'hard to get'. One evening, having worked late, and alone with this pragmatic Adonis, over coffee the conversation turned to the realms of married love and how, having once experienced this normality of life the wartime absence of the physical side of love, could be harmful from a point of view of frustration alone. Before long Maudie and her colleague had agreed that the resumption of normality was overdue for both of them and what better time and place than the present. 'I will go and fetch the necessary equipment and I have a lovely book. Perhaps you would like to prepare yourself while I am away,' said the scientific officer, and left the Nissen hut. Maudie didn't know quite what to do to prepare herself. Suppose she took her frock off and someone from the Camp came in? No, she could always 'prepare' herself at the height of passion, although she doubted any passion would arise somehow. She wondered why she still stayed, possibly because the next bus that could take her home wasn't due for an hour. The book her lover would produce she imagined would be a book of poetry. How touching; she would never have associated him with such tender sentimentality.

Her lover-to-be reappeared. He was wearing a dressing-gown underneath which Maudie could glimpse swimming-trunks. How clever! Of course he would appear to any outsider to be on his way to the shower. But he also had two pillows and a blanket, a bottle of whisky, two glasses, a book, and what Maudie thought was the strangest thing of all, a small metal cash-box with a key in the lock. He spread the blanket on the floor, placed the pillows side by side and motioned Maudie to take her place on this 'couch'. She was now having great difficulty in keeping her face straight. The officer poured a minute amount of whisky in each glass saying he thought it would help them to relax. It was hardly a teaspoonful. Fortunately Maudie didn't like whisky but it crossed her mind, even though she would have been suspicious had it been a large tot, that here was a mean man. He put the glasses on the table, the book by his side, and then methodically 'opened the box'. 'Oh, God,' thought Maudie, 'surely he is not going to ask me what I charge?' But out of the cash-box he extracted a sheath, which he placed by his side on the blanket, then locked the cash-box again and placed it tidily by the side of the glasses. 'Now for Browning,' giggled Maudie to herself as her passionate friend opened the book. He began to read, half to himself, a sort of manual on 'how it should be done'. Maudie suddenly felt a long way off and the next ten minutes were like an unfeeling dream; she could have gone to sleep and felt she wouldn't have been missed, for even his kiss was like placing blotting-paper on blotting-paper.

When it was all over, and she only knew this was so when the officer poured her another minute nip of the liquid which she always understood was guaranteed to 'put fire into the belly', he put his arm round her and said, 'Now comes what I always think is the best part of love-making.' ('God, is there more?' thought Maudie.) But no, the best part was 'the chat' on the occurrence after the occurrence, according to her lover. Maudie was silent and for the first time believed what a friend had told her some years ago. This friend apparently could sleep anywhere and had told Maudie that once she had 'dropped' off at the passionate heights of her husband's love-making. She had awoken, with a start, to find herself alone in bed and thought, 'Now, something was happening, what was it?' Realising what a terrible thing she had done, what an insult to a dear lover, she had gone in search of her husband and then upset him further by bursting into peals of laughter. He was sitting in his pyjamas by the dying embers of the sitting-room fire, moodily smoking his pipe, but he had put on his bowler-hat, to keep warm!

CHAPTER ELEVEN

Homecomings

Both Susan and I were excited at going home. She gave a great sigh as the train drew into Liverpool Street and it seemed as though she had been holding her breath for this moment. I gave her a hug which evoked a blush and a smile. She was a quiet thoughtful child, one of those children who are 'no bother'. My only worry was her extremely poor appetite and dislike of milk.

My old mum and dad were at the gate of the house at Forest Gate waiting excitedly to greet us. Dad led Susan into our dining-room which was shining from Mother's exertions. In the middle of the floor was a blackboard and easel and chalked on the blackboard in Dad's best printing were the words, 'Welcome home, Susie.'

Susan was soon away to play in the road with her old friends. It seemed strange that they had been separated all over England for so many, many months, yet they all knew each other instantly and within a few moments it was as though they had never been separated.

VE-Day was announced and the war in the Far East seemed a long way away since none of the men in our road had been in that theatre. Great bustle and activity took place as the wives began a gigantic spring-cleaning and first-aid repairs to their war-scarred houses. A street party was organised and we expected Chas home on leave at about this time. He was now on the borders of Yugoslavia and Italy with the Venezia Guilia Police Force, very busy as usual (he was a magnet for work) requisitioning hotels for the army. He would take an inventory of one hundred rooms, in record time, entirely by himself.

I eked out my meat rations in order to get Chas a nice piece of meat for the day of his arrival home. I don't know why I made sacrifices for this meal really, for whilst in the Police Force he had had the services of a marvellous Chinese cook who one day placed before him sixteen grilled kidneys, and this at breakfast time! But he would be hungry after a long journey and as we had been separated for three years a meal would help to overcome our initial shyness with each other. I was quite convinced we would be painfully ill at ease for the first few days after his homecoming.

About an hour before he was due to arrive I fetched Susan in from a lovely game she was having with her friends. She took a dim view of this, after all she had never known her daddy really. She was quite content with the adults she already possessed. At last, both mother and daughter looking like models from a magazine, we sat quietly waiting. And we waited, and waited and waited. Finally, assuming Chas would not be arriving that day we both changed into our 'everyday' clothes. Susan rushed back, with great glee, to her friends, and I went upstairs to sit with my parents. All my excited anticipation had dissolved and I felt suddenly irritable.

Susan and her friends had knocked several times for all those things children like to keep worrying one for, possibly they keep returning to see if Mother is still there, so that irritable at a further knocking I rushed down to the door saying bad-temperedly, 'Well, and what is it now?' and there was Chas. We gazed at each other for a minute without speaking and then he said, 'I've knocked several times, you know.' This remark after the time Susan and I had spent dressed up waiting for this very knocking! He then continued, 'Is that dirty-looking child in the green coat out there, mine?' 'Susan *is* wearing a green coat,' I said. 'But she can hardly be dirty.' I felt furious that neither of us had retained our model garments. Susan came in as we went into the dining-room (Chas and I had not yet greeted each other with even a kiss). Chas and his daughter eyed each other like protagonists. 'Here's your lovely Daddy at last, darling!' I said brightly, anxious to erase the previous moments of his arrival and start afresh with a real welcome. Fortunately she allowed him to kiss her and I helped Chas off with his pack, suddenly in a dither, not knowing whether to talk to him first or march Susan off to the bathroom for it appeared by the look of her she had been playing 'mud pies'.

However, all the jobs got done and after our meal I prepared Susan for bed, while Chas went up to see my parents. We only had one bedroom, although it was a very large one, and I had purchased a single bed for Susan which I placed in the far corner of the room. She had slept with me for the greater part of the war during the air-raids and eyed this new bed with reluctance. 'Is he going to sleep here then?' she asked. 'Yes, darling,' I said. 'For ever?' she queried in a horrified tone. I thought it expedient for the sake of a peaceful evening with my beloved, to tell a white lie. 'No,' I replied reassuringly, 'not for ever,' and I added quickly, 'Daddy's going back to another country in two weeks' time.' Fortunately this satisfied her and she was soon fast asleep. I changed hastily and donned a glamorous-looking housecoat in green and gold brocade. This had come from Persia and had been a present from an American officer to his wife, but she had deserted him for someone else and in a state of emotion he had given it to me saying, 'Here, Towser, perhaps it will do something for you when your husband returns, I admire women like you who have carried on so cheerfully and loyally while their husbands have been away.' 'It's an ill wind,' I had thought at the time, rather callously. The officer felt his wife had no reason to desert him, no raids or shortages in America to cause her to do such a thing.

I lit the fire, for not only would it be more welcoming and easier to relax with each other in its flickering light, but I thought Chas might feel the cold on an English summer evening after living in such warm climes. I placed two arm-chairs by the fire, and awaited his return from above. He removed his arm-chair from the fireside and sat in it by the window. 'He's more shy than I thought he would be,' I reflected. He seemed to be staring at me in the firelight. I was just racking my brains for something nice to say to him when he arose suddenly from his chair. 'At last.' I felt all warm and loving at his approach. But no, he switched on the light and said belligerently, 'Now I'll see the books.' 'Books,' I stammered, 'I didn't know you liked reading.' 'No, the bank books, the savings books,' he went on as I gazed stupidly at him. Book in the singular would have been bad enough at such a time, but books in the plural! I was furious, all my loving, welcoming mood evaporated. Everything had gone wrong, I was sure it wasn't my fault, and thus ensued, on our first meeting after the toil, stress and misery of the war, a fierce argument. Chas calmed down first and it transpired that 'someone' in his mess, or the officers' mess (he must have been a hypnotic beast, I was sure) had warned the chaps that their wives had held the reins for so long they wouldn't relinquish them easily, and unless a man 'put his foot' down on arrival home from a financial view, he might become a second-class citizen in his own home, and not the man of the house as he had been before the war further emancipated women.

However, the argument seemed to clear the air and remove the last traces of our shyness with each other, and after a drink both very tired (at doing nothing exciting) we retired to bed. As I took off my housecoat I thought, well, perhaps bed is the right place for making love. No sooner had Chas put his arm round me than a little voice came from the corner, 'Can I come in your bed, Mummy?' Deciding quickly to myself, 'Well there's another day tomorrow,' I was on the point of saying, 'Of course you can, darling,' when Chas said, quite sharply I thought, 'No, you cannot, just close your eyes and go to sleep.' Of course Susan began to cry and I said to Chas, 'You shouldn't snap at her like that.' I went over to her, and for the sake of peace and quiet I whispered that if she closed her eyes and tried to sleep I would buy her something extra-special the next day. This seemed to be the right approach and we heard no more from her. I was glad Chas hadn't heard my bribery and corruption promise to her for he would have been very cross I am sure.

Back in bed, to make a fresh start, I tenderly took Chas's hand but with an unearthly groan he thrust my hand back at me. This inhuman noise heralded the start of ten days' illness for him. He was very poorly indeed, the doctor diagnosing either gastric flu, dysentery or a foreign bug. Mother made up a bed for him in her spare room in case of infection. He recovered, but the illness left him with severe palpitations so that he was unable to exert himself in any way! Finally he visited a military doctor and thankfully his heart returned to normal. I felt I was being punished in some way for my unpatriotic wishes at his first army medical. Now that the war was over surely his heart wasn't going to have its own back on me? However we had at least a couple of happy days before he returned to the Continent, and his leave was still not 'wasted' one might say, for by the time he returned home demobbed I was already large with our second child.

We had visited the hairdressers towards the end of his leave. The salon was run by a married couple, who, I thought, knew me well. The ladies' salon was on the ground floor and the men's on the floor above. I was ready to leave before Chas and sat in the passage with the proprietress waiting for him. As he came down the stairs she said, 'Here is your son, won't you be glad when he is home for good.' So I looked old enough to be his mother, and he had spent nearly two weeks as an invalid! I looked at Chas and he was actually 'grinning' (quite a feat for him) and as we went down the road he burst into laughter. I shook off his arm and wished he had been wearing a revolver for I might have shot him on the spot. And to think a month previously I was sure I would be spending two weeks of rapturous bliss. At the very youngest I must look fifty!

There was no comfort from the family, either. Mother giggled and Amy inspected herself in the mirror, her look confirming, yes, Dolly looked even older than her older sisters. The hairdresser's remarks really cast me down so that when I went to the station to bid farewell to my youthful warrior, I looked and felt like crying and Chas departed beaming like the sun. This was his last departure, his next homecoming would be permanent. How different from his first departure, then I was smiling radiantly and he almost in tears. His leave had not made me impatient for the future and I had to learn all over again that some things cannot be planned. I addressed my next letter to him 'Dear Son,' and his speedy reply was a passionate apology for his laughter at the hairdresser's remark. He had only been laughing because I had taken it seriously. The hairdresser was of course mad, his officer, whom I'd met at the station had been very smitten with me. 'I had no idea you had such a striking-looking wife,' he had said to Chas, 'and what a brilliant sense of humour.' I wished I could have remembered what I had remarked to the officer; I remember I thought him quite a dish. I cheered myself up by deciding that I was one of those people with a 'fixed age' when I reached the age people assumed I was, those around me would grow more ancient while I stayed the same.

Some time after Chas's final return he was offered a position with a shipping company. He possessed the necessary qualifications, there were excellent prospects with this company, and never having been one hundred per cent keen on canvassing or salesmanship, he took the position with the S.S. Co. And we installed a telephone—the first members of the family to arrive at such affluence! We longed for it to ring after the engineer left. But silent stayed the bell. Until we were asleep that night. Chas answered it and returned to me white-faced. A 'dreadful' voice had said, 'Your life is in danger.' 'I must phone the police,' said Chas agitatedly. 'Whatever can they do?' I asked, and persuaded him to come back to bed. I started to laugh when I thought of his terrified expression and he was a bit sulky about my laughter. Suddenly, just as I was dozing off he sat up in bed and said in a delighted tone, 'The man didn't say "Your life is in danger".' 'Oh, good,' I said, happy for him. 'No,' he went on. 'I realise now what he did say.' 'What was that then?' I said, now quite interested, 'Your *W*ife is in danger,' he said triumphantly. Now he went to sleep with a smile and I lay awake quite worried.

Chas liked his job, Susan liked her school, our neighbours were friendly and life was pleasant while I was waiting for my next baby to be born. After the miserable intervening years we seemed to have enough to smile at. We had two girl neighbours whom I liked very much. They were real characters. Ivy and Nell. They had been lifelong friends, had married two brothers, both quiet and gentle fellows, and now they shared a large house half a dozen doors away from us. Nell had a voice mightier than an 'Ada Larkins' and whatever part of the district her young son Peter was playing in, her 'PETER' always reached him. Their day's work finished, the girls would station themselves on the wall of the front garden, the railings of all gardens in the road having been removed 'for the war effort'. Here they would sit and pass the time of day with a joke to the homecoming men, most of whom were a little bit shy at the evening's public greeting, but Chas always had a smile and a ready word for them and when I was preparing his meal at evening-time I always knew of his approach before he reached our house because of Nell's serjeant-major's, 'Evening, Charlie—had a good day, boy?' They were cockney girls of the old school, with no shyness or fear of anyone. They gave me hours of amusement and I was 'Dolly' to them before I'd been in that area more than a few hours.

Nell's son was in the same class at school as Susan and at the end of the first year after the war the children brought home their school reports. I always met Susan from school and Nell's son walked home with us. The reports had been rolled out on a green jelly pad and the words 'Nature Study' had come out faintly 'Nature'. As I asked Nell, when we were comparing the reports, 'And what has he got for Nature Study?' before I could say the word 'study' Nell looked at her son's report and said, for all the world to hear, 'Nature? Well, I'll tell you, Dolly, if he's anything like his father, it's bleeding 'ot.' It took me a long while to explain to her what Nature Study really was. 'Well,' said Nell, obstinately, 'he don't bleeding well need it, not if he takes after his father!' His father was so quiet and gentle I could hardly believe Nell's description of her husband.

Chas never appeared interested in 'bank' books again and we decided to spend the war-time savings on modernising our house. We were fortunate in obtaining the services of a 'master-builder', the strangest master-builder I have ever seen. He was small and slight, yet possessed the strength of a Goliath. He was a cultured man with a lovely voice and an Edwardian manner of speech, and with an old-fashioned courtesy. He was the first builder I had met who did not make me feel as though my house was falling down. Whenever I had asked for an estimate for decorating etc., the builder or decorator had always looked round tragically, tutted, making me feeling I was asking for a miracle, and finally, while the estimater was 'hesitating' on the price to be asked, I would jump in with profuse apologies for daring to invite a real 'craftsman' into what they always made me feel was a 'dump'. But this new man I had engaged was like one of the Three Musketeers in his gallant treatment of me. His first job was to put a picture-window down one side of the kitchen wall and he would bang away at the brickwork singing in a lovely voice or reciting poetry. He would say, 'If Madam would be so kind as to journey to the front gate we might ascertain as to whether the building inspector approacheth.' Like a madam I would gaze up and down the road, and on my return would describe a man who might be walking near the house, and my little craftsman would put his hands together and gaze up at the sky in supplication and say, 'All is still well for that is not he.' What action would have been taken if 'he' did 'approacheth' I never knew.

My mother liked my little craftsman, perhaps because he was like a little faun in his leaping and springing movements, perhaps because she liked his singing or poetry. Doubtless he brought out the maternal in her and he brightened visibly each time he saw her. She would make hot scones for his morning tea feeling he needed feeding up. My father, on the other hand, was a little frustrated by my Musketeer, possibly because he couldn't fault his work. My father, a craftsman of the 'old school', would say '*craft*sman' with such an expression of disgust when workmen were employed by any of the family, but D'Artagnan was perfect so Father avoided him whilst he was working on my house. But as soon as the little courtier had left for home in the evening my father would scoot downstairs and inspect very carefully every inch of the work, and return silently to his books. Finally my father accepted the newcomer as a member of the craftsman fraternity and in a subtle manner eased his frustration through ploys against Chas.

Chas had decided to cultivate the back garden. It was a mass of trees, lilac, firs, etc., and at the bottom of the garden there were a William pear-tree and a cherry-tree. He removed all the trees with the exception of the fruiting ones and soon had rows of vegetables planted. Chas thought he detected a slight air of coolness in Father's manner towards him and I was designated to discover why. Of course, Father paid his rent, he was 'entitled' to half the garden. It was difficult to apportion now that it was planted and in any case Chas had no idea that 'the old Adam' lay unsatisfied in Father's breast. He couldn't understand why Father had the urge to dig and plant when he would have been presented with as much of our crop as he needed. However Father was given the piece of garden near the fruit-trees.

Now Mother had already bought and planted, in the small front garden, a forsythia bush of which she was very fond. Chas, reorganising the front garden, dug this out and laid a lawn. Looking forward to the birth of my second child and the modernising of the house I was not really aware that the removal of this bush had upset Mother for she had said nothing to me, always wanting a peaceful atmosphere around her. Whether my father knew this I don't know, but one of his garden bonfires 'accidentally' destroyed the cherry-tree, and I began to feel like Piggy in the Middle for Chas would complain to me one day and then Father mumble about Chas's gardening capabilities the next. Father, all innocent, would dig and plant where Chas had already 'put his mark' and then Chas would return the compliment. Father gave up first, possibly bored with gardening, and filled his whole patch with everlasting spinach. Fortunately this flourished always so his pride was salvaged and an uneasy peace restored.

Then Chas, always the unsatisfied farmer, bought some hens which caused my father to criticise 'backyard fowls' and the disease and pests associated with them. He hated these cackling birds but would have calmed down and probably accepted them peacefully when he saw the lovely brown eggs. But Chas, fired by the success of his first venture into poultry-keeping, bought a cock. This grew into a magnificent bird and Chas was immensely proud of it. He just loved all the chickens and gave them all names which my father seemed to think revealed an unmanly streak in my husband. Now, for some mysterious reason, this cock hated my father, and if Chas had gone to work without locking the run it would take off and fly across the garden towards my father screaming whenever it saw him. My father would not admit that he detested this cock because he was nervous of it, indeed he never galloped into the house when the bird made a bee-line for him, but he did put on a sort of 'Olympic walking-race' run, and he always took a stick with him into the garden. Finally Chanticleer's days were numbered for he flew at Susan one day, and at last I put my foot down. My father ate the roasted cock with happy relish, but Chas sadly refused any.

All this excitement amused D'Artagnan no end and now my father had become quite friendly with him for the little man had gone so bravely to Susan's aid at the time of the bird's attack, and indeed, saved her from a nasty injury. One evening Susan called from the bedroom that someone was sawing underneath her bed. At first I thought she must be dreaming but suddenly I heard it, a sawing and a scrambling, down in the cellar. We had arranged to have a new kitchen floor and in the old wooden floor, by the side of the cooker, was a hole about the size of a penny. And from this hole emerged the nose and teeth of a RAT! I was absolutely terrified. Chas fetched the long carving-knife with the narrow point, sharpened it to razor-like proportions and laid full length on the kitchen floor intending to stab and perhaps impale the intruder and so kill him, but every time the wretched creature poked his nose through the hole Chas 'jumped' and always missed it. We had a sleepless night and I longed for the morning when the 'Rat' man would call.

He came, a giant of a man, and whilst, in the manner of a surgeon, he laid out his paraphernalia, he informed us, so very modestly, of course, what a dangerous mission he had chosen in life, only the brave could survive his calling. D'Artagnan, from the top of his ladder, gazed down with sceptical grimaces at this ratty V.C., and we waited with baited breath while our brave hero descended into the bowels of the house. He was wearing a sort of face mask and had thick gloves on his hands and a cudgel in one of them. We waited for the verdict. He led us to believe that we had an influx of the terrible rodents and first of all he must tempt them and reassure them. He would feed them with good food and when they were happy and 'at home' with their surroundings and had become trusting creatures, then he would poison the food. The thought of the next few days with a happy family beneath me so terrified me that when the brave man had departed, D'Artagnan went down and inspected the cellar. 'As I thought, Madam dear, there is only one rat there, I caught a glimpse of it, it is crippled, ill and old, and has probably been turned out by the other rats from some other place.' We had a small air-hole on the outside wall and my father thought it had probably come into the house that way.

The next few days were torture to me, although I was very glad I had two men in the house day and night. My father went down the cellar hoping to catch the rat, but he never saw it. At last, after the rat's repast had been poisoned, came the great day of salvation. The V.C. dressed himself for the battle which he led us to believe, would ensue. Well he convinced me of his bravery under assault, but not D'Artagnan who announced to me that morning he was sure of the rat's demise, the poison being a deadly one. Sounds of battle and war-like cries emanated from the cellar and presently up came the rat man with his hands behind his back. 'Don't look, missus,' he implored. 'It's not a pretty sight.' I made coffee for this marvellous man and he left with an aura of a job well done. D'A. watched his retreat down the road and then galloped back to the dustbin. Coming back into the kitchen with joy shining from his dear little face he announced, 'Just as I believed, Madam dear, "rye-goor morteese" had set in.' It really had been an outcast from its tribe, old and unwanted. My father somehow blamed Chas's chickens for the arrival of the rat and their days too were numbered.

CHAPTER TWELVE

Saturdays with the Cheggies

Saturday afternoons at Forest Gate were lovely interludes and red-letter days of the week for Mother and me, for then members of the family, who lived near enough, would come home to visit. The children would find their way downstairs to Susan, and I would find my way up for tea with Mother and my brothers and sisters. My father and Chas were away at their football- or cricket-matches, and we loved their absence for this afternoon. For one thing Chas could never be at home doing anything without wanting me constantly by his side. He could never 'find' anything and always seemed to need a mate to pass him various implements for the job on hand.

Amy couldn't understand what she thought was my 'servility' to Chas and my pacifying replies to him if he was irritable about anything. But, like my mother I would 'give points away for peace'. I detested arguments over things that didn't really matter in life, but Amy, to me, seemed to enjoy arguments, or perhaps it was that her pride would not allow, what she thought was subservience, to another human being, least of all man! Her husband, James, was a gentle fellow, warm and affectionate to her. He would never argue with Amy, but just remain quiet and calm at times of stress, and this probably frustrated her. Too, she was not afraid or timid of rows as I was; I always worried that arguments or quarrels might become physical, whereas Amy was brave and would attack the strongest.

One Sunday morning Jimmy, feeling warm and loving towards his wife made tentative advances. Amy, anxious to get up and on with the cooking and housework, repulsed him. Thereupon Jimmy began to sulk and Amy, furious at this, picked up her corsets and began to belabour Jimmy with them. 'No more, Cheggie dear,' he cried. 'I am sorry, I won't sulk again. Amy laughed at this incident while the rest of us looked disapproving. 'I am afraid she's like Dad's mother,' said my mother sadly. Mother wasn't against a woman standing up to a man, that wasn't the reason she had disapproved of Grandmother Chegwidden. I learnt from a whispering Agnes that our paternal grandmother, a small and elegant body, like Amy, was not only a spitfire, but an enjoyer of 'love'! She actually let it be known that Grandfather, another gentle soul, was not 'satisfying' enough for her. No wonder Mother was disapproving. Apparently my grandfather, late home for lunch, had registered a mild complaint, or perhaps just a remark, about his meal. It was his favourite, pork chop, roast potatoes, sprouts and celery. Granny removed this instantly from him and sat at the table eating it herself with great relish and enjoyment! Mother used to say to us, 'And he never complained about anything ever again.'

I had seen my grandmother once when I was a little girl, before my younger sister was born. She was old and ill and Mother took me to visit her. She lived with my Auntie Dot at Tooting and I thought Tooting was a beautiful name for a place. My mother took with her a large William pear. I had never seen anything so enormous. Mother wrapped it carefully in tissue-paper in a tiny carrier-bag. I knew my grandmother must be very very ill for Mother to take a William pear with us for it seemed to me my mother treated this pear as though it was somehow different from the fruit on the stalls. It must have had a special significance and although I would love to have taken a bite from the side of this lovely plump fruit, I wouldn't have liked to have been poorly in bed at the time for it would have told me I was very ill.

We went into a downstairs bedroom in the Tooting house. In bed was a tiny woman with glittering dark eyes. They looked searchingly at me and a husky voice said, 'So this is Wal's youngest, this is your Dolly.' Just then the sun sent a beam of light into the dark room. It seemed to wrap itself warmly round me and hide me from my grandmother, yet her voice went on, 'A little golden angel to kiss me good-bye.' Mother said quickly to me, 'Run out into the kitchen and fetch Auntie Dot.' In the kitchen Auntie Dot sat me in a wooden armchair and said, 'Sit still, there's a good little girl,' and she ran out of the room. Mother came to fetch me after a long time and we went home from Tooting on a tram. Grandmother couldn't have been there, I remembered, as we had passed her bedroom when leaving the house, for the sheet was right up over the pillows. Somehow I knew she hadn't eaten that enormous William pear, yet Mother didn't have it with her any longer. My mother would always say there is nothing like a perfect English William pear when someone is ill, and I couldn't understand this when young, for the invalids Mother seemed to visit with her special fruit always seemed to pass on at the sight of it.

I saw very few of my parents' relatives when a child as I was at the tail end of a large family. There were too many of us to pour into an aunt's or uncle's house and of course it would have been impossible anyway for my parents to have afforded the train and bus fares. My mother's relations were all country folk, Dorset, Wiltshire, Hampshire. All sweet innocent folk living a peaceful life working on farms or country-mansion gardens, caring for animals, happy in nature. My father's people, on the other hand, were quite different. On his father's side the Cornish sailors and merchants, but on his mother's side, a different race altogether. My grandfather was Grandmother's second husband, so it was whispered. Her surname was Rose and she was related to Jewish business people. My eldest brother and sister visited many of these exciting people every week-end when they were young, but I was grown up before I really heard about them.

There were family names of Nathan, Levy, Skolinsky, Folingfan (or Pholingphan) Rose, and I did hear once that through the Levys there was a Rothschild! Uncles Nathan, or Levy, had a public house in Cable Street, Stepney. Aunt Temperance (what a combination if it went with Skolinsky or Pholingphan!) had a sweet-shop in the Mile End somewhere and Alftruda, a cousin, had a 'posh' restaurant at Windsor. We had an uncle Constantine in America and I used to think we may be an ordinary family, but we certainly possessed some unusual names. We gained two more unusual names with Chas' grandmother for she was Miranda Minerva.

But there, although I envied my paternal granny and my sister Amy for their bravery, they both possessed extra gentle husbands. It was all very well for Amy to think I could emulate her retaliatory behaviour. Chas would never raise his hand against me in an argument, but I had the feeling that had I struck the first blow his pride would have been so thoroughly injured that my blow would have been instantly and 'lovingly' returned. His reactions were so quick he wouldn't stop to think what he was doing.

No, much as I might have wanted to emulate Amy, we were

entirely different characters. For one thing I really found nothing ecstatic in life, though I was always wishing to, whereas for Amy, everything *was* ecstatic and I envied her intense enjoyment of life. Even when she was away in hospital she turned this into a drama. After her first child was born she began to suffer poor health. My mother insisted Amy was not taking care of herself, but her first baby was a large child, always hungry, and it seemed really as though he was too robust for as tiny a mother as Amy was. A friend of mine saw Amy and her offspring out walking one day. Amy, always an expert needlewoman, had made pram-coverings etc. unusually luxurious for the neighbourhood, and her baby's hand-made clothes would have been outstanding even in the West End shops. She, my friend, said the baby, in his lovely perambulator, looked much larger than Amy. 'Mind you,' said my friend, 'Amy looked a cocky little bit.' I assumed my friend was jealous, but Amy *was* getting thinner, Mother was getting worried about her and finally the doctor thought Amy should go away to Brompton Hospital for he thought she might be developing T.B. Mother was horrified, there had never been such a dread disease in any of our families, ostrich-like she was sure it was either a wrong diagnosis, or she blamed Amy's other connections for this shadow which had come upon the Chegwiddens.

Amy left Brompton Hospital. Mother was pleased the doctor had 'ticked Amy off' by saying, 'You have a large healthy family. You don't want to spoil your mother's record, do you?' There fore, according to us all, 'it was Amy's own fault'. Off she went to a convalescent home in Surrey, where, as usual, Amy had a fine time, chopping down trees and enjoying weekly socials (it was a mixed home). She borrowed my little portable gramophone, the first in the family, which I never saw again. Mother was very sorry for James, because Mother always felt if a married man was denied affection, which was his by married right, he would fall by the wayside, for men, in Mother's mind, were different glandular creatures from women. I think, personally, that Amy was the exception to Mother's rule, and I think Mother was secretly proud of Amy, even though she thought her like our paternal grandmother. Amy said mysteriously, 'You don't want to worry about Jim.' We thought this just bravado for there was nowhere at the convalescent-home, or so we thought, where gentle Jim could even kiss Amy, except on arrival or departure, but Amy was one day describing to me the lovely church there. Apparently this church had a small chapel in the corner. Solid walls at the bottom, but glass half way up. The chapel was really for mothers with babies so that, as it was sound-proof, mothers could listen to and watch the service through loud-speakers, or ear-phones perhaps, and a restless child would not disturb the worshippers in the main church. Now Amy and Jim would attend the service, but in the sound-proof chapel, and Amy once said, 'No one can see, from the main church, what is "going-on" below the solid part of the chapel walls.' This sentence spoke volumes to me, for as one horrified member of the family said, 'Surely, no one would "co-opt" in a holy place!'

Alfred, Marjorie's husband, was now demobbed and one afternoon we were listening, with great interest, to the army tales Chas and Alf were swopping, when Amy, probably bored by it all, or perhaps a little chagrined that she possessed no returning hero, interrupted with, 'It was much worse for Jim in the Home Guard, and he never received a gratuity or lovely underclothes.' Marjorie's face became scarlet with indignation. 'Gratuity!' A choking pause. '*Lovely* clothes! . . . Do you think two sets of long pants of inferior quality, a suit off the rack, and £78 compensates a wife and child for the long separation from a loved one?' 'Well,' said Amy defiantly (I knew she'd never give in), 'he was never in the firing line.' This I thought was hitting below the belt, for Alfred had been in the Syrian desert with the front line of communications. He had been terribly ill (gravely so), and was even, after demob, a pale shadow of his former robust self. Jimmy had been the M.O. in his Home Guard troop and thought his whole war had been somewhat on the hilarious side. Amy had worked at various jobs, so that with Jimmy's full and increased pay from his reserved occupation, and Amy's salaries, the £78 Marjorie received for five years' separation and hardship was only cigarette money compared to Amy's affluence. But some civilians were like this towards serving soldiers. Chas, abroad for three years and one of the soldiers of the First Army who had missed embarkation leave (Churchill apologised publicly for this rushing away of the men) was once on seven days' leave after many many months, yet two or three people said, when meeting us out walking, 'On leave again? You always seem to be at home!'

Marjorie, near to tears at the suggestion that her husband was not a battle-scarred warrior (even though I had said to Amy, 'Monty was very pleased Chas and Alfred were on the same side') was somewhat cheered by my father's sudden interest in her flaxen locks. 'Your hair looks a treat, Marjorie,' he said. 'I never remembered how fair you were.' Naturally Amy resented Father's spontaneous compliment on Marjorie's hair; considering he never remarked on the attraction of any female, the compliment was the greater and more sincere. But Amy was silent now, possibly to atone for her previous remarks, but she knew and I knew and Marjorie knew that when she, Marjorie, had told my father her extra brilliance was because she had been in the sun rather a lot in the country, it was untrue. Peroxide was the operative word. But she looked so attractive that I decided I would try to merit the same spontaneous compliment from my father. Unfortunately I had no idea that this beauty liquid had to be diluted. I used the whole bottle, my scalp stung and I had white spots on my fingers, but pride feels no pain, and I went upstairs after my hair had dried. Possibly it was because my hair was a different colour to start with, but it had turned a most peculiar shade of marigold. When I entered the room to the astonished silence of my brothers and sisters, my father's yell came first, 'Christ, here's another one of them that's been in the bloody sun.' He had realised instantly that he had been 'conned' by his baby, innocent little Marjorie.

My brother David often came with his wife Lydia to our family get-togethers and they both joined in the fun. David had been discharged early on in the war, through deafness. Again Mother would not have it that his debility was due to family deficiency in any way. Someone had told her that men go deaf when attending to big guns during the war, and this she claimed must have been the cause! I was happy for David, who like so many men, were not born fighters. Like them he would have made the best of Army life, but he was a sensitive chap and civilian life was the best for him, and in spite of his deafness I was glad he was out of the war.

Lydia had a great sense of humour and loved the thrust and parry which went on between everyone. My father said he could hear us all when he was a long way off whilst returning home from his football-match. He would say, 'It sounds like a Jewish Parliament.' There was plenty of opportunity for the family to 'criticise' me for I often absented myself from the roaring debate and fierce arguments, for when many of the grandchildren were present, ever worried they would quarrel, or even fight, I would spend much time tearing up and down stairs to the back garden, settling arguments among the children, pouring oil on troubled waters, but ostensibly 'watching' my own offspring's interests.

There were so many differing personalities amongst our children.

Margaret, Winifred's daughter, a very intelligent child, was a born leader, so who should be 'teacher' in their games but she, Susan, rather on the timid side, was one day delegated by the 'teacher' to be the 'naughty' child in the class. On one of my visits downstairs she was obviously upset about something. 'It's that Margaret teacher,' said young David, Lydia's son, in a hoarse and conspiratorial whisper. 'She's too strict.' 'Oh dear,' I said, all worried. 'Don't worry, Auntie Dolly,' said Dave's young son, suddenly the champion of Susan and me, 'I'll kick the teacher, when she ain't looking.' Since he was as in awe of the 'teacher' as much as Susan was, I thought him extremely brave, but at the same time deemed it diplomatic to dissuade him from this course of violent action, not only did I not relish his chances, but I wished to avoid any dissension from the mums and dads upstairs. Young David would do anything for Susan. One day they were playing tea-parties. It was a cold day and I refused them real water to play with. Therefore when I went to call them I was surprised to find they had 'real' tea. Little David had 'obliged' Susan by 'weeing' in the teapot. I prayed they had only pretended to partake of this unusually brewed concoction.

Cecil, in the Navy, seemed to thoroughly enjoy the war. He was a Gunner's Mate and had some exciting times, especially when chasing the *Graf Spee*. He had done well and was Chief Petty Officer. He was a champion pistol shot in the Navy and loved target-shooting. He once got into the King's hundred at Bisley.

We saw little of my brother Charlie and his wife, Edith. He was now 'mine host' at a public house in Essex. He, like Amy, seemed afraid of nothing. He was extremely popular with his customers, being 'Charlie' to all. A transport-driver I met in Suffolk during the war was very excited when he discovered Charlie was my brother, he said he'd never forget him, he was a real character, and he never knew what Charlie would be up to when he arrived. Once he was flying a huge kite and another time practising all-in wrestling with an all-in wrestling customer who wanted more experience for a forthcoming bout.

Brother Arthur once stayed with Charlie and his wife for a week-end, but was horrified at something which happened in the saloon bar. Charlie's wife, Edie, asked Arthur and his wife what they would like to drink. She then asked several other people present and after serving the drinks presented the bill to Arthur with a 'That'll be £ . . ., Arthur.' She had a dead-pan face.

Charlie was once on a luxury passenger-liner, where he was a plumber. At the Sunday morning service the 'tape-recorder' which played the hymns, broke down. The Captain tried to start the congregation off with a well-known hymn, couldn't get the note to start it, then the padre tried; he too failed, and so it went on through the officers, the bosun, all hypnotised into failure, all men's voices trying different notes to get the 'off' until finally one of the passengers struck the right note. Charlie said it was one of the most hilarious incidents he had witnessed. Jimmy James, the comedian, wasn't 'in it'.

I was unable to back Marjorie up in her recriminations about Amy, for Amy was to take care of Susan while I was in hospital for the birth of my baby, now imminent.

At last the day came when I knew I must journey to the local hospital. Chas was at work, my parents upstairs having their breakfast. I picked up my little case, kissed Mother good-bye and left the house. I felt very lonely as I walked to my assignation and then I met Ivy. 'Good God, Dolly,' she said. 'You can't go alone, nobody does.' She ran her little son home to Nell, caught me up and took my case. The maternity wing of the hospital was attached to a work-house-cum-old-people's-cum-mental home and as we entered the gates a vacant-looking old man approached us. He was dressed in the grey cap and clothes worn by the inmates of such institutions. He literally beamed at me as he said, 'You'll have a lovely baby, missus, just like I was.' 'Oh, Christ,' said Ivy indignantly. 'That's all the good wishes you'll need, Dolly.' This amused me and I was laughing as I entered the building.

I was interviewed by an aloof and extremely haughty doctor. One glance at me seemed to overcome him with boredom. 'What's the story?' he drawled in upper-class tones. His manner and mode of speech robbed me of any importance and stupidly I stammered, 'I think I'm going to have a baby.' He glanced quizzically at the hovering Sister and between them flashed the message, 'An idiot mother, this.' In the same bored manner he examined me and pronounced, 'No, you are not having a baby, well, at least not this week, go home and attend the clinic next week.' I went home feeling thoroughly disappointed, definitely not in the mood for resuming domestic chores. Mother tutted sympathetically and made me some tea but within an hour I was almost running to the hospital feeling frightened at having to stop and hold on to anything at hand to support the stabs of pain. Again I met my beaming old, grey friend and this time he was delightedly surprised. 'Another baby already,' he enthused. 'That *is* good.' He took my arm with great joy and led me to the entrance.

This time Sister saw me, 'You'll just have time for a quick bath,' she said leaving me alone in the bathroom. I undressed, Sister had insisted on the door being left open, and a woman who was passing put her head into the room and hissed, 'You want to be careful, my baby was born down the lav, don't you let them give you an enema.' Although I hardly believed her and would not have been brave enough to refuse such medication, I decided not to bath for baby would have had no chance if born under water, and I just dampened the towel for the sake of appearances. Sister reappeared and said brightly, 'Now come along and enjoy your lovely lunch.' Since I couldn't imagine obtaining enjoyment from even Coq-au-vin at that stage I certainly couldn't eat the stale-looking corned beef and salad spread out before me by the side of a bed in a huge ward. The pain seemed to come in wave after wave and in the end I was unable to stop my groans. I was trying hard not to spoil lunch for the occupant of the bed by whose side I was sitting.

'Call the nurse,' she said. 'They didn't ought to have left you here like that.' 'No,' I said, 'they know what they are doing.' However this lady suddenly screamed out, 'Nurse!' in blood-curdling tones and I was led, like a lamb to the slaughter, to a bed in the side room. 'Ring if you need anything,' said the nurse. Whatever does she mean, I thought, 'need anything'? 'Well, if you get panicky,' added Nurse quickly leaving the room. Hardly a moment later came a pain so searing and so prolonged I pressed the bell. In came a differently dressed nurse, a midwife I supposed. 'What on earth are you ringing the emergency bell for?' she said irritably, but there was no need for me to reply for within a few minutes my son was born. 'Dash,' she said, 'I suppose you know you've torn yourself.' 'I *am* sorry,' I said apologetically and then I wondered why *I* was apologising, for I certainly wasn't mistress of my fate at that time.

I was now wrapped in a blanket, and sitting in a wheel-chair, I was deposited at the bottom of a flight of stone steps by an elevator in the corridor. The lift was marked 'out of order' and a passing nurse ordered a passing porter to take me up to another floor. 'I'm the porter for *this* floor,' he said, so I remained static. Finally another porter was fetched. He too was the wrong floor porter and the two of them began a heated debate as to their different floor duties. Finally when the argument became too fierce and the word 'union' was mentioned, two nurses and Sister assisted me up the stairs. 'Bloody men,' said the woman in the next bed when she heard about the fracas. 'They want to have the kids, then they'd know all about it."

She was such a jolly woman. She said to me, 'Look at this,' and pulling back her bedclothes she exposed one white leg and foot and one black leg and foot. Apparently when her labour pains started she had been scrubbing a muddy floor. Shouting to her husband to fetch the ambulance she put one leg into her kitchen sink and washed it, but things became too urgent for any attention to the other leg. 'Keep your bloomers on, missus,' said the ambulance-man in the hope that that would slow things up and he could get to the hospital in time, but nothing can stem nature and her baby son was born in a terrific rush. She wasn't allowed to feed him for the first few days. The complications caused by his speedy arrival meant that he had to be kept in a tilted cot. Eventually he arrived in the ward and we all cheered. 'Is there any Chinamen in your family?' my jolly neighbour asked when she first saw my son. Well, he certainly did have an oriental look about him, he was pale in comparison with the other red-looking babes and possessed no wrinkles.

On the other side of me was a pretty girl whose baby had died at birth and I wept silently for her. At feeding-time she would pretend she was asleep and I thought it was brutal to keep her in a ward with all the other victorious mothers. It may have been therapy to harden her up to face the outside world but we all felt such sorrow for her.

Towards the end of the first week trouble struck our ward. Whether the virus, or germ, was brought in by a soldier on leave I do not know, but mothers and babies went down with a type of gastro-enteritis or dysentery. The ward was closed to visitors, disinfected, and we all felt on an island since we were not allowed to fraternise round each other's beds and the ones who had contracted this miserable disease were placed in further isolation at one end of the ward. The sisters and nurses worked day and night and when I contracted it I felt like dying for the pain caused one to faint away. Finally I recovered and was allowed to take my baby home which surprised some of the mothers, for the hospital had decided to keep the babies for a time in an isolated nursery. Sister had said to me, '*Your* baby will be all right,' and since she gave no other explanation the other girls thought I must have some influence they didn't know about. But he progressed well and was an easy baby to care for.

VJ-Day had come, the war was over, my husband was safe home again, I had a son and a daughter, a house with a garden, a husband with a job he liked. What more can a woman desire?

CHAPTER THIRTEEN

Chicken-feed

Food was still rationed at the time of my son's birth and other goods were difficult to obtain. Perambulators, for instance. However I advertised and for eighteen pounds, which my parents thought was an unheard of sum of money, I purchased a second-hand pram. It was a huge affair, a Rolls-Royce amongst prams, navy blue with a sort of rail running round the bodywork. It was the same make as the royal prams! 'Your mother never felt the need of a bassinet with the ten of you,' said my father! His disgust at the price of this pram never abated, he just couldn't forget it.

But Mother did have a little wicker-work affair for the last four of her children. I think Sister Kathleen from Poplar All Saints Church acquired it for Mother. It was a dangerous two-fold contraption which would close like a concertina, literally trapping the occupant, if it was pushed down the stairs or pavement too quickly. Amy told us of the time she and my brother Len were in charge of Marjorie, the then occupant of this wicker trap. Adjured by Mother to walk slowly, never run, when taking Marjorie for a walk they completely ignored her advice and chasing out of Tunnel Gardens one day, late home for dinner, they upturned the bassinet throwing little Marjorie on to her head on the pavement. Passers-by picked Marjorie up and extracted from Len and Amy the solemn promise that they would 'tell their mother what had happened' for their little sister must be taken to the doctor, it was such a nasty blow on the child's head. Of course they didn't tell Mother and when Amy related this episode, with glee, at our weekly get-togethers Marjorie said, 'No wonder I'm supposed to be the simple one of the family, I see the reason why, now.' 'Whatever makes you think such a thing?' replied Amy. 'As a matter of fact I was thinking only the other day, it was Dolly of course, Len and I were taking out in the little wicker bass. We didn't mind taking her out because she was always smiling, whereas you were such a miserable child.' 'So that's my reward for trying to spread a little sunshine around,' I said to Amy feeling furious I had been denied the medication I certainly must have needed after such a fall.

Mother, now getting old, was so very anxious to take my son out in this beautiful perambulator. Amy had embroidered a beautiful white cover for it and Mother was keen to be the object of admiring eyes. She was so looking forward to saying, 'This is my youngest grandchild, William,' for she liked the name. I had wanted Nicholas but Chas hated it saying it would become 'old Nick'. Then I plumped for Dominic, Miles, or Rupert, but finally gave in and settled for William.

I dressed William in his best white woollies, polished the perambulator till it shone, then I had to dash away to collect some washing from the garden for a neighbour had called to say my line had broken. When I returned, Mother had left for her walk round the houses. I sat at the sitting-room window awaiting her return and became hysterical at what I saw, and I called my father. He too began to laugh and then he said, 'Don't tell your mother for God's sake, she felt such a grand lady pushing the posh perambulator.' Hanging over the front of the rail which went round the body of the pram were Mother's pink Twilfit corsets. They looked enormous and the lace laces dangled almost to the pavement. They must have somehow got caught on the rail when Mother was taking some laundry upstairs, and Father hadn't noticed them when he was pushing the pram outside the house ready for Mother's take-off. She'd had a lovely walk and everyone 'had been so happy' to see her. I managed to slip them off the pram when I opened the door to her. She would have been so humiliated to discover them and I had to warn different people who had noticed them, not to mention the corsets to my mother. One stupid woman said she thought Mother was going for a walk to 'air them off'.

It was lovely living with my parents, for in that way I saw my brothers and sisters and their children when they came to visit Granny and Grandad. My brother Len always kept us amused. He had risen to the rank of major in the army, no mean feat for a boy from the East End. He'd been on the raids to the places where it was suspected the Germans were working on 'heavy water' which was connected with the dreaded atom bomb, and he had a fund of anecdotes. At his final interview with the brass hats on the occasion of his promotion one of the interviewers was a crusty old colonel. 'Speak up,' said the colonel, 'I can't hear you.' Up spake Len. 'Don't shout,' said the crusty colonel. 'I'm not deaf.' He had to give an impromptu lecture on 'places abroad I have seen'. Fortunately he'd been in the Navy and he spoke for fifteen minutes on '. . . miles up the Orinoco' which apparently had the assembled company enthralled. My father was so proud of Len. Len laughed at the 'visiting' card, or 'menu' Chas had brought home from abroad. It stated, 'One egg and chips, ten shillings.' 'Cor, that was pricey,' said a laughing Len, then Chas turned the card over and on the back was printed, 'And two saucy girls will dance to you.' 'Were they good dancers?' asked Marjorie.

Chas's family visited us too, but without the fund of amusing anecdotes my family had a store of. Robin had not 'enjoyed' the army, an intellectual type, I knew soldiering would not be his cup of tea. I think he was left very much to his own devices, for, as he told me with a laugh, 'route marches were not for me'. I often wondered if it was not a ploy of his so that he could return to his books in the quiet of his hut. At one time he was stationed abroad within a few miles of Chas, and decided to visit him on his day off. They went to a camp show but Robin was unable to sit with Chas as Chas was a sergeant and Rob a private. I thought this stupid but Chas said 'discipline' had to be maintained. I think he'd got the wrong word, for Rob wasn't the type to start a revolt. He was once in charge of the switchboard. It was a dark and stormy night with the rain lashing down. The Sergeant phoned instructions to Robin from the other side of the camp, quite a way away and Rob replied, 'Righteo, Old Boy.' Minutes later a soaked and furious Sergeant appeared in the switchboard room shouting at Rob, 'Understand, Private, I am *not* your Old Boy.' Rob and his wife Olive ran a grocery store in North London. They worked like slaves and had very little time off, but on Thursdays Rob had his men friends in for cards, always a must with Chas and his family, all great card-players. Chas was always late home on these Thursday nights but I always sat up for him. I liked to welcome him home again and in any case I enjoyed the quiet of the house when my family were safe and asleep. I liked a late night myself, for I hated going to bed whereas Chas was always weary before 10 p.m. But on this fateful night he was later than usual and midnight came and went and there were still no footsteps on the path. I heard a noise upstairs and crept up to investigate. Mother was rubbing my father's shoulder. She was in a temper at my father requesting such a service at such an hour. 'Why didn't he mention earlier that he had a touch of rheumatism?' she said irritably. 'Rub it well in,' my father was saying. 'Rub it well in.'

I went downstairs to renew my vigil, amused at my father's expression which had cropped up several times in my life. A friend of my brother's had told him of the M.O. they had when he had been in the army. A really nice chap, obviously an aristocrat out of the top drawer, and yet he tried hard to speak to the chaps in their own language. It was a London regiment so many of the fellows were down-to-earth cockney lads. They were to be sent abroad and the M.O. was very worried that because it was the first time so many of them had been to foreign climes they would not fully comprehend the dreadful dangers of disease were they to associate with 'ladies of the town'. He began the lecture by advising the chaps to have nothing to do with ladies they didn't know; in that way they would return home as pure as they were when they left their native shore. Realising this sound advice had very possibly fallen on many deaf ears, he began his lecture proper. He produced a tube of ointment and squeezing the tube he displayed to the assembled audience its contents. A vivid blue wode. He then proceeded to inform 'you chaps' that if they found it impossible to go through the war abroad without 'a little affection' then they could obtain this indigo dye magic salve from their M.O. It must be applied to the er . . . er . . . The M.O. obviously thought if he used the medical terminology for the appropriate parts of the male anatomy, the chaps would not fully comprehend, and so conscientious was he and so anxious that his men should remain F.F.I. (the army term for 'free from infection') that with great embarrassment he said, in pseudo cockney tones, 'Rub it well in, rub it well in, round the er . . . cock . . . and er . . . balls some minutes before the er . . . get together.' There was great amusement amongst the chaps as one would imagine and the ribald remarks which followed, about Indian warriors, etc., and the air was blue with risqué jokes. I thought it a pity the colour was blue and wondered why the army could not have made it colourless.

It was now two a.m. and I was more than ever worried. Something dreadful must have happened to Chas. There was a sudden loud knocking and a continuous ring on the front door-bell. Immediately my worry changed from relief to 'How inconsiderate he is to make such a noise at this time of night. He must know my parents and the children are asleep.' I dashed to the door ready to attack him in a hoarse whisper, but as I opened the door a light almost blinded me. There stood a policeman, dressed in despatch-rider's clothes, bearing on his head a huge lamp, like a miner's light. 'Is Charles William Scannell resident here?' he asked severely. 'He was,' I stammered. 'May I have his present address then?' he said, taking out a notebook. 'Oh, he still lives here, but where is he now, has there been an accident, please tell me, I'm not silly.' 'Just a moment, Madam,' he said, waving his hand for 'hush'. 'Let us get the facts straight first. Is he, or is he not, living at this address?' 'Yes, he is, but tonight he is in North London.' Now frantic I said, 'He's dead, isn't he, you are afraid to tell me, but I must know what has happened.' Realising that he must come clean with an hysterical female he said, 'Madam, your husband is in good hands at Leman Street Police Station.' He paused, then he said, 'Now may I know what took your husband to North London?' 'I think he went by bus,' I said. 'Yes, of course he went by bus, the trains don't go there.' He was now more muddled up than ever and was sure that not only had they apprehended a criminal but had discovered a nest of criminals possibly. Why else was this woman being so evasive, for it was obvious he thought I was. I was getting more worried than ever, what was Chas doing in a Police station? 'I can tell you one thing,' I cried. 'Whatever he's done, he's innocent.' And then followed my testimonial to Chas's character. He was nothing more or less than a saint before I had finished my speech. 'Well,' said the policeman, 'try not to worry.' Then when he saw my tragic face he knew what an impossible request he had made, and he said, 'Physically he is fine, no doubt you will be informed of what is happening in the morning.'

I sat up all night going over and over in my mind what could possibly have happened, I almost collapsed by the fire thinking of his undergoing a sort of third degree. Of course it was a case of mistaken identity. Should I try to telephone? But who would I ring? The police obviously would have closed lips. I couldn't bother Rob and Olive, they probably knew nothing about it. The policeman's loud knocking had surprisingly not woken the household. I would fight for Chas. He would have the best lawyers in the country. I fetched my Post Office Savings Book—

11*s*. 9*d*. Of course, I had spent my all on the house. I couldn't think what lawyer I could get for eleven and nine-pence.

In the morning an unshaven, worried and tired Chas arrived home and part of the sorry story was revealed. Rob, who was a registered dealer in chicken corn, was overstocked with it. No one in North London seemed to want it and it was a nuisance in his busy shop. That evening he had said to Chas, 'Look, this will soon be off the ration, would you like to take some home with you?' Ah, thought Chas, if I have corn I can buy some more chickens. In addition to a sack of corn he gave Chas half a pound of butter and a quarter of tea. Rob and Olive and their charming son Geoffrey had been to lunch with us the previous Sunday and had brought no rations. 'I can't go to the bother of going down into the shop again tonight,' Rob had said, not wanting the bother of weighing up two ounces of this and four ounces of that, so that although the half a pound of butter and the quarter of tea was more than they had eaten, or drunk, the quantities made up for the other rations consumed.

That night on his way home from cards at Aldgate, Chas encountered a police-car standing at the kerb. The sack being heavy Chas innocently rested it for a moment right by the doors of the car. These immediately opened and a charmingly kind voice (Chas said it was lovely and welcoming), called, 'Good evening, sir.' Chas replied, just as politely, 'Good evening, officer.' 'May I ask the contents of your bag?' enquired the officer. 'Yes, certainly,' said Chas (an unknowing lamb to the slaughter). 'I have some chicken corn, half a pound of butter and a quarter of Reddings tea.' 'And,' continued the voice, still kindly, 'May I ask where you got all this from?' The penny dropped! Chas realised that what he had was on the ration. He had broken the law, but what worried him more, what was worse, his brother had technically broken the law and he would be involved. The first thing in my boy scout's mind was to protect the innocent. 'Well,' said Chas, 'I am sorry to admit it, officer, but I stole it all.' The voice lost its warm kindly tone, but still polite it said, 'In that case, sir, will you come to the station and make a statement?' I wondered what the policemen would have thought if Chas had said, 'Well, I'd rather not.' But of course into the car went Chas. (He said they were very nice and called him Charles all the time. I think he appreciated this politeness.)

By this time he was, of course, terrified, his head whirling. He had branded himself a thief. Perhaps he wouldn't be in prison long, but he must try to name some place from which he had stolen the corn, other than his brother's. Alas for the criminal mentality.

He made several different statements (I wondered at that stage in Chas's confession whether my despatch-rider had returned and was describing the criminal's wife!) but in the end settled for the first one, 'He had been playing cards at his brother's and, while his brother wasn't looking, he had stolen this very large bag of poultry food together with the butter and the tea.' The police couldn't seem to get clear from Chas how he left his brother's premises without his brother being curious as to what was in the sack-like bag which had not been in his possession when he arrived for his social evening. Chas, being an honest citizen got absolutely muddled up, and of course the more worried and muddled he became, the more like the criminal they suspected he was did he appear to his blue-coated kindly-voiced friends. His hand shook as he finally signed away his character and he remained in the Police Station while the law sped to Rob's shop.

Rob was furious that the police should wake him up in the middle of the night. He and his wife worked very hard, for their shop was extremely busy and successful. When he learned that Chas had said he'd stolen from his brother, he was even more furious. 'He's a b.f.,' said Rob. 'It's typical of him.' Rob made a statement and said to the departing policemen, 'I should think you'd be busy enough searching for the big black market boys.'

In the end the whole police station was laughing, all except poor Chas, of course. At midnight the poultry-food had been taken off the ration because there was such a glut of it, and the half-a-pound of butter had melted in the warmth of the police station, no doubt singed by Chas's conscience. As for the quarter of a pound of tea, it wasn't worth the bother, for Rob could prove that on the way to our house the Sunday before he had met a policeman friend and in conversation had said to his wife, 'Oh, hell, I've left our rations on the kitchen table.'

'Now I suppose they have your finger prints,' I said accusingly. 'What does that matter?' replied Chas, and waving his arms dramatically he continued, 'I am not guilty.' I was just about to start a long stream of recriminations for my night of torture but his dramatic, 'I am not guilty!' recalled to my mind the judge with a reputation for brevity. The criminal in the dock had dramatically waved his arms to the court and called out in heart-breaking tones, 'As God is my judge I am not guilty.'

Replied the judge, 'He's not, I am, you are.' Therefore I thought I should let well alone, I would always have something to fall back on in any future domestic argument!

But I couldn't leave well alone and the more determined I was that Chas shouldn't keep chickens again, the more determined he became to own these stupid birds. I was fighting a lone battle, for eggs were still rationed and as Mother said so many times (probably coached by my father), 'Eggs contain enough nutrient for a meal, and with potatoes, we could manage in an emergency,' and my father insisted that Chas's eggs looked better and tasted better than the shop eggs with the little lion on them. My mother would come down each day with a new 'sales' quote on the subject of 'our feathered friends'. Her greatest quote, and one which she thought most daring and modern was, 'If a man is denied his pleasures at home he will seek them away from home, such is the nature of man.' Rob presented Chas, not only with his large supply of poultry-food, but with a pest-proof bin in which to keep it. This bin was about four feet high, made of heavy metal. It also had a strong hinged lid. And four stiff-legged females took up residence at the bottom of our garden. The only concession made 'to keep me quiet' was the promise that these ladies would lead a cloistered existence. No male bird would ever ruffle their feathers. So Daisy, Dora, Elsie and Ethel lived a peaceful life. Whether their nun-like existence was a happy one I neither knew nor cared. I couldn't even tell them apart.

CHAPTER FOURTEEN

Happy Ending

In the years after my son's birth Chas found no fault with his life. He liked his job in the docks. Thursday was still card night at Rob's, week-ends gardening and football, and we managed on his wages (only just). Never over-ambitious, he was always more intent on conscientiously carrying out the job on hand. No war now, the years, for him, stretched away peacefully in the foreseeable future. Family crises were usually solved by the time he arrived back on the scene.

On the other hand I was restless. I didn't know why. I didn't know what I wanted. I told myself I was happy caring for my children, indeed I wouldn't let anyone else look after them, and was always ill at ease when they were away from me. Mother suggested I take a night off now and then and visit the cinema, but I couldn't concentrate on the film. Suppose they woke up and I wasn't there. So that when events occurred which could have been tragedies, but which were by a miracle averted, I couldn't relax, and although my 'Thank God' was fervent, I couldn't forget and would go over and over the occurrence in my mind. Thus, when friends and relatives hinted that I was a little over-protective of my children I felt utterly enraged. I felt that some parents were fortunate their children arrived home safely after they, so it seemed to me, carelessly dismissed them from their sight. Thus I felt it unfair that three near-disasters should have happened to my children. I had no ambition for them, only ever wishing for them a 'normal' contented life, which was an anomaly, since *I* was never content and subconsciously was jealous of and resented my husband's contented acceptance of his lot.

One Saturday afternoon I went happily up to Mother's flat,

to join my visiting sisters. The men were away at football, Susan was safely at tea with her little friend near by. William, then about two, was playing in the back garden. He was a child happy in isolation, always digging and inspecting holes. He was never any bother. The garden door, a large heavy one, was bolted, the front door as well. He couldn't reach the bolts. No harm could come to him.

The family left just after an early tea and I went to call my son in. There was no sign of him. I just couldn't believe it. The man next door was digging a very large hole in his garden. 'Have you seen William?' I asked, a little worried, but not too frightened at that stage for Susan might have come in and taken him to play, though I knew this was hardly likely. 'No,' said my neighbour, shortly. I thought he looked strangely serious. I dashed to my neighbour's house. Of course, Susan and her friends hadn't seen William. The doors were still bolted, he couldn't possibly have left the back garden. The man next door had now filled in his large hole and was raking it over. 'Are you sure you haven't seen William?' I pleaded vainly. 'He's missing.' Still the man just said, 'No.'

My mother called from the window, 'I've seen Charlie and he's running off to the Park, he thinks William has wandered off there.' I knew he couldn't have wandered off, I knew he couldn't have left the garden, and with my throat dry and parched and a feeling of utter desolation creeping over me I decided to go to the Police Station. I don't know why I opened the garden door and looked down the garden again. Had I not searched it thoroughly and called my son's name so many times? In the growing dusk two white spots caught my eye. Two white spots on top of the poultry-bin. What were they? I tore down the garden and head downwards in the bin was my son, his face not quite buried in the corn. How he reached the top of the bin had yet to be worked out. I had yet to go over in my mind the 'ifs' that had either saved his life or taken him from us. The lid had remained open a couple of inches because of the depth of corn remaining in the bin. I yelled to Mother and carried the little limp figure into the house. His face was wet, his eyes closed, but he was still breathing. Mother bathed his face and put some milk on to warm whilst Father rubbed his grandson's hand and said, 'Come on, old chap, wake up.' At last William opened his eyes and said to me, 'I kept calling for you.' And where was I, upstairs chattering away without a care in the world!

Such a load of guilt was too much for me to bear and

immediately I transferred the whole of it on to Chas's shoulders. He was to blame. He should never have left the bin-lid open. I had never wanted the wretched chickens. I was just longing for his return when all my torments could be unloaded on to him. I knew I would attack him when he returned from the Park. He looked so white and shaken, so helpless and so worried when he appeared, that at long last I burst into tears. 'Now, now,' said Mother. 'All's well, that ends well.' Once she had started on these trite sayings she thought of many more applicable proverbs, her last one being, 'Accidents *will* happen in the best of regulated families.' She unearthed a box half full of Christmas crackers and we wore paper hats for a celebration tea. The door-bell rang. Wearing my paper hat I opened it to the man next door. 'Did you find your son?' he enquired solicitously. 'Yes, thank you,' I replied. 'He was in the chicken-bin.' He walked away looking dazed and I knew I should have to explain to his wife one day what had happened, otherwise they'd think me a mental case. 'Who was calling?' asked Chas. 'Oh, Mr . . .' I replied. 'He wanted to know if we'd found William, and was there any way in which he could help.' 'He's a very nice man,' said Chas. 'Isn't he,' I agreed, 'I've always thought so!'

Before I had recovered from that terrible afternoon, Susan failed to return home from school. More searching took place and I was fortunate enough to find someone who knew she'd gone home with one of the 'bigger' girls from her school. I went to the girl's house. 'Oh, no,' said the mother. 'She hasn't been here.' She then turned to her daughter, a girl older than Susan and rather hefty-looking, and said, 'You don't know where Susan is, do you, have you seen her this evening?' 'No, I haven't,' replied the girl. Something in the girl's eyes stopped me from leaving quickly and I glanced round at her as I went down the path. Did she look at the garden shed? 'What do you keep in your shed?' I asked the mother. 'You surely don't think she's in there,' was her indignant answer. Just to show me I was crazy she unlocked the shed, and there was a frightened Susan crouching in the corner. The girl had decided to 'kidnap' her. I was furious with the girl, furious with the mother for saying, 'She was only playing,' furious with Susan for her timidity, and furious with myself for ever longing to be a mother. 'I expect you'll have more worries to face yet,' said my mother cheerfully. 'You hold too many post-mortems,' added my father.

Of course my mother was right, there were many worrying days ahead. Somehow I could cope with illness, even at the most awful time when Susan contracted polio I kept my nerve and unswerving faith in our marvellous doctor. When a child is ill there is so much one can do but when a child is 'missing' then there is the despair of utter helplessness. I was always so careful to ask child visitors, 'Did their mother know where they were?' 'What time were they supposed to be at home?' Chas or I would take them safely home. I always hoped other parents would do the same for me, but alas, this was not always so. When Susan was eleven and at grammar-school, a schoolfriend's father called at the school by car, and collected his daughter and her friends for an impromptu party at his house, some miles away from our district. Children are unpredictable and Susan probably thought she would be home in a couple of hours, but the party went on until ten p.m. and then the father just bade the girls good-night with no enquiry as to whether they had their bus-fare, or whatever. Susan arrived home at 11.30 p.m. having had to walk a couple of miles through a seedy district. By this time I had alerted the police and was almost in a state of collapse, and the father who had thrown the party just shrugged his shoulders.

I often thought it might be a good idea to shuffle babies up at birth, or to exchange them, so that one could lovingly take care of a child without the awful tugging of the heart-strings. A child would perhaps be free then from a parent too dedicated or too emotional. Little knocks, or hurts, or slights, which appear to upset one's offspring mightily at the time, are often forgotten by them very quickly, but a mother sometimes remembers them and perhaps worries about them for many a day. My children were rather serious characters. Susan seemed to have no bother with her homework and I was never asked to assist, which was a relief for I had left school at fourteen, I had passed no examinations, she was much brighter than I had ever been. Her favourite subject was English and she was a writer of interesting essays. A special essay was to be written for some occasion or other. Susan spent one evening on it, writing speedily and took it to school, without suggesting I read it. The next day she returned home, in tears, and passed the essay to me. In red ink across the bottom of the page the teacher had written, 'Well done, Mother'!

However, I *was* responsible for the next tragic happening. She was a very poor needlewoman. 'She takes after you,' said my mother. 'You always sewed with a red-hot needle and burning thread.' The needlework mistress had given the girls a sampler to work. First of all they must embroider their names across the top of the special material. Susan's progress was slow and the mistress suggested she bring it home to work on it in the evenings at a spare moment. For the first time in her school career she elicited my help and I was determined to rise to the occasion. By the time I had finished, the material contained large holes where I had sewn and unpicked many times. Susan was in tears, Chas furious with me for ruining the sampler, Mother looked at me as though I was a criminal and my poor father rubbed his bald head helplessly. 'Pretend you've forgotten it at the next lesson,' I instructed Susan cravenly. I would buy some more material and I knew Amy would willingly assist us. She just hated to see children despondent. I journeyed far and wide but could find no identical material and in the end Susan went to school with the holey sampler. 'Oh dear,' sighed the needlework mistress. 'Couldn't you have asked your mother to help you?' I was glad Susan admitted it *was* all her mother's work, for the mistress laughed and arranged for Susan to take Latin instead. She probably thought she would be fighting a losing battle against heredity. (I had been wandering about all day worrying.)

But not all her school troubles dissolved so easily. At the end of the first year, examinations were held. They were told these examinations would be run on the same lines as the G.C.E. This would give them experience for the future. A different form-mistress attended as adjudicator while the examinations were in progress. Having completed her papers, Susan sitting in the front row sat waiting for the bell to ring. Glancing round she saw that some of her friends in the back row, having also finished, were reading library-books. Her satchel was by her feet and from this she took her library-book. Suddenly the adjudicator rose from her seat and approached Susan. 'What on earth do you think you are doing, girl?' she demanded. (She had only to examine the book and she would have discovered it had no bearing at all on the examinations.) 'Do you not know this is dishonest?' Picking up Susan's papers she said, 'Your papers will be cancelled, your marks nil, and no doubt what you have done will be mentioned on your school report.'

Susan contained herself until she arrived home and as I opened the door she burst into tears. 'I wouldn't have that,' said the other mothers, for the girls had told of Susan's ordeal. 'Lots of them were reading, and I am sure they would all say so.' In the end, because I was not brave enough to face her tutor I wrote of our distress at the happening. I received a cool reply. Rules were rules, and this experience would help Susan at the real G.C.E., which was right, but I did need a bit of understanding. It was shortly after this that Susan contracted polio, and while she was in hospital I was told that her headmistress was very disappointed Susan's mother hadn't even let her know of Susan's progress! I wrote to *no one* fearing I might infect someone.

If the headmistress thought Susan a problem child, me, an over-fond mother, one could hardly blame her considering all the circumstances, and bearing in mind the fact that she didn't know me. Evidence against Susan, albeit circumstantial, seemed to be building up.

Susan recovered from polio and returned to school. It had been snowing and icy cold and some of the girls had made a slide in the playground. The headmistress, naturally, was angry that her girls should have partaken in such a dangerous pastime and the edict went out 'Any girl sliding . . .' On her first morning back, because of a visit to the doctor's for a clearance certificate, Susan was a little late and crossing the playground slipped on this ice and hurt her arm. She kept this injury to herself, I don't really know how, for on arrival home she was in such pain we went straight to the hospital. Her arm had been broken and was put in plaster. Because of the icy conditions of the road the doctor thought she would be safer at home until the weather eased. I telephoned the headmistress who said, 'Well, I am so sorry, but I did warn the girls of the danger of sliding on this ice.' I tried to explain that Susan had not been disobedient, but I knew it was useless.

Life continued uneventfully during William's pre-school days. After lunch I would take him into the nearby park to play, and through these regular visits I became friendly with another mother, a girl of about twenty, whose son of eighteen months, her first child, played happily with William. We would chat about everything under the sun, confiding in each other all manner of things we wouldn't have told another soul.

One day I told Vicki that a sister of mine had remarked that I was developing quite a bristly moustache and had the positions been reversed, my sister, rubbing her perfectly bald countenance, had stated 'she' would definitely have done something about it. Possibly I had always been a downy chick but I had to admit that of late my face was developing a hirsute appearance. Vicki seemed quite pleased at this. Apparently her husband had taken of late to gazing at her more intently than was his wont and she sadly agreed that her downy skin might, when she was *old* like me (this made me feel like an old shaggy creature) turn as bristly as mine. But, small words of comfort, it would be worse in her case because she was a brunette, whereas my moustache and beard were gloriously golden!

Vicki took from her handbag a newspaper cutting which stated 'superfluous hair removed instantly and permanently with this new and miraculous invention'. In our low state of mind at that moment we decided we would attend at this miracle-worker's clinic. My mother, very disapproving of the venture, interfering with nature and all that sort of discourse, grudgingly said she would have William for the day. My father inspected my face and said, 'Don't worry, gel, it's simple, just set light to a rolled newspaper and run it over your face every so often. Why,' he added comfortingly, 'I knew an old lady once who needed a blow-lamp for her face!'

On a cold winter's day with a vicious east wind blowing, we started our adventure. My heart was beating with fright, but as we had Vicki's extra lively son with us, looking after him at least kept my mind off my forthcoming operation.

Our destination was some miles away in one of those new towns which were springing up. Everything was different, the roads appeared either unnamed or with such strange names. The bus conductors had no idea, and neither did the various passers-by we enquired of, where this 'beauty' parlour was, so that two hours after we should have been 'done' and 'gone', we finally arrived at the scene of our eventual transformation.

There was much new building taking place and our 'surgeon' was housed temporarily in an old building due for demolition. It had been bought by the Development Corporation and they had installed a temporary canteen. We were gasping for a drink and hungry for something to eat, but decided we would partake of refreshment as new beautiful matrons, not as hairy monsters. We entered a tiny suffocatingly hot room and were surprised to see that our benefactor was not an efficient surgeon in a white coat but a motherly-looking lady in skirt and cardigan. She even possessed the large 'mum's' bosom of my childhood. She was just completing a session on a most beautiful looking blonde which cheered us up enormously for the blonde rose (treatment completed), with a happy smile; it was obviously a true advertisement, painless.

Vicki's small son being restless and wanting to dash round

the small hot room, I motioned her to take her seat in the swivel-chair. I would amuse the little boy and keep him safe for I felt the small room could be a death-trap for an unwary adult let alone a lively youngster. The small electric-fire was placed in the middle of the floor, the lead having been lengthened, in a most amateurish manner it appeared to me, by many different coloured pieces of wiring and lying, nearly atop of this wobbly-looking fire was an enormous poodle dog. Hitherto I had only seen pretty toy poodles, but this one, black, appeared as large as a labrador. I tried to overcome my nervousness of this dog and restrain my charge at the same time so that I really didn't pay too much attention to Vicki in the treatment-chair. The motherly lady chatted away to us telling us of all the hairy clients she had cured. One girl even had treatment for a hairy chest! And we gathered that our lady was in much demand by the hospitals. This was all reassuring and presently Vicki, treatment completed, took her small son from me and said she would meet me in the Canteen after my treatment. 'Did it hurt?' I whispered to Vicki. She nodded in a negative way. I thought her smile a bit stiff-looking and she seemed to have tears in her eyes. I assumed, as she had smiled, that she was feeling pleased about her treatment, the tears being relief that she would now remain attractive to her fussy husband.

I sat confidently in the chair but at the first jab of the needle I let out a terrific yell, startling my electric 'mum' and waking the dog who crawled towards me and placed his large hot head in my lap. 'Oh, God,' I thought, 'he's been trained to restrain clients like me, the cowardly ones.' I apologised profusely to the lady operator, said I hadn't been expecting any sensation, I would now know what was coming and would not yell out again. Famous last words, but true, well almost, in my case, for instead of yelling I slowly retreated downwards on the swivel-chair. At one time we were both almost supine. 'Oh my aching back,' said the lady. 'You really must sit upright, or we'll both be on the floor.' She did add that my roots were tenacious, it was the type I was. I sat upright as she said something to her dog and then she said, 'I've never known him to take to anybody like he has taken to you.' At this compliment the dog climbed the chair and laid full length on top of me, his head resting on my chest. He was hot, heavy, and a bit smelly but I was too weak with hunger and thirst and perhaps too terrified to request his removal. I placed an arm on top of him and he snuggled down to sleep happily. Tears were running down my face as the hairs round my mouth were treated. The half-hour seemed like years and my good intentions flown out of the window, I flinched, and more easily now because of my heavy load, slowly sunk backwards. Suddenly there was a terrific crash, chair, Dolly, Dog, and Torturer floundered about on the floor. The dog barked furiously at me, the fire wobbled dangerously and my lady rose painfully and switched the fire off. She brushed herself down and said wearily, 'I don't know whether you would like to make another appointment, providing I can fit you in. I am so much in demand these days.' For the sake of appearances I made an appointment for two months ahead knowing I would not keep it.

I said good-bye to Dog who now growled at me, and went to find Vicki. The canteen was closing and I said to Vicki, 'Why didn't you tell me it was so painful?' 'I daren't, dear,' she said, 'because if you'd known you *would not* have had your session.' The depressing thing about it all was the fact that it wasn't one miraculous session as the advert suggested (perhaps we hadn't read it thoroughly) for Vicki, very bravely, attended for almost two years. I never went again, for Chas had said about my furry face, 'I assure you, it never bothers *me*.' I arrived home frozen, blotchy, and bad-tempered, and the next day my face was swollen and I was beginning a nasty cold. I felt nature was so unfair. My sisters had no such bother. I blamed Mother for allowing my brothers to play barbers with me as their sole customer in the days of our childhood.

Now it was time for my son to commence school. Actually it was over time. The schools were so overcrowded that he had to wait until well after his fifth birthday, then he had an additional two-months' delay because of the fear of infection in connection with Susan's polio. I had no fears for him. He was so adult in his speech, so exceptionally knowledgeable on subjects other children of his age could understand. Modestly, oh so modestly, I thought, 'He will race ahead, he will be no problem.'

Happily we left to enrol him on his first day. It seemed like bedlam in the little classroom, crying children and mothers loth to leave, 'prolonging the agony', my father would have said. 'Welcome to our school, William,' said the teacher, on hearing his name. 'Is it always like this?' he asked the teacher. 'No, thank goodness,' she said with a laugh. 'Oh, that's a relief,' said my William, 'for the noise is already giving me a headache.' She looked surprised at his manner of speaking and gave him a little squeeze. Happily I left, it was obvious he and his teacher were going to be friends.

Some neighbours and I had arranged to take it in turns to collect the children and I was anxiously waiting at the gate for him at lunch-time. A sad-faced mother handed me my son with a note from his teacher. William's face was white, his eye swollen and his forehead bruised. The note just asked me to call that afternoon if possible. William announced he had a bad headache and putting him to bed I left Mother on guard whilst I went to see his teacher. The teacher was terribly sorry about William's injury, but we both agreed it was 'just one of those things', a misunderstanding. All types of children make up a school as all types of adults make up life, and the large tough leader, or bully type, boy in William's class had said to him at play-time, 'Coming to play wiv us?' This invitation was really an honour and perhaps might have made a difference to my son's school life if he had said, 'Not 'arf.' But always a gentle child he had observed rather rough treatment being meted out by the giver of this invitation, and my son had said, 'I would like to play if you will avoid physical violence.' It was the last three words of this sentence which caused the breakdown in schoolboy relationships, for immediately on the defensive the large tough boy had replied, 'You ain't bleeding well calling me names,' and wham, had landed a punch on my son's unready face. Even this blow would have not caused the injuries he sustained, but unprepared, unsuspecting and off balance he had fallen and caught his face and head on the cement piers which supported the school playground wall and railings. The teacher seemed relieved when I agreed no one was to blame, and I hoped it wasn't the first of many misunderstandings. She was a dedicated teacher, with a deep love for all children, and I remember her with gratitude.

Great excitement pervaded the household when our first television-set was installed. 1950! What an achievement and what a popular family we became. I loved every minute of our film-shows. Children in the afternoon, adults in the evening. During the school holidays the children would inspect the TV programmes and after lunch I would place the chairs in a row, make lemonade and cakes, and quiet reigned for two hours. William had to have a seat on the back row near the kitchen door for something about the printed words on the screen seemed to worry him and he would dash off into the kitchen until the words had faded from the screen. Since his 'visits off' were many, if he sat in the front row there were yells and groans from the other children, 'Don't keep going across the screen, William.' 'Mum, look at him now, he keeps getting his head in the way.'

Every evening, promptly at 7 p.m. my parents would appear and take their seats. One evening when Chas was late home and I was feeling irritable at his overcooked meal, I unkindly tutted at my parents' extra-prompt arrival. Immediately my mother said, 'Come, Walter, we are going back upstairs.' My father who was in the middle of choosing his seat said, 'What is the matter, has the set broken down, can't they get the man to repair it?' 'Come, Dad,' Mother said more firmly. 'I will explain upstairs.' He followed her looking puzzled and getting a bit cross at her slow explanation. I heard her say, 'We do not go where we are not wanted,' and I felt a real cat. I felt too guilty to face my mother and before he started his meal Chas ran upstairs. I heard him say, 'You know what Dorothy is like sometimes, she doesn't mean it.'

My father needed no further coaxing, he was downstairs in a flash and I gave him a quick résumé of what had gone before in order that he could follow the programme. A few minutes later Mother appeared with a sort of Queen Victoria look on her face and Chas whispered to me, 'Whatever do you want to upset your mother for?' I don't really know, perhaps I was bored by the interminable cowboy films my father loved, they all seemed the same to me. The goodies, the baddies, the sheriff, the posse, the hangings, the lynchings, the coming of the railroad, the Indians. Eventually as my father could never get enough of such films the rest of us soon found other things to do in the evening. I would sit upstairs with Mother with my book or knitting. Sometimes when I went downstairs at bedtime I would find Father asleep in the chair. I would turn the set off, wake him up and try to convince him that the sheriff had really got his man and the lynching had been foiled by the posse. Sometimes I don't think he believed me and he looked forward to the next time in the hope the film would be repeated.

My mother was somewhat worried by my bouts of sudden irritability even though she realised they were often caused by my anxiety over my children's lack of appetite. She felt their non-eating and non-drinking habits would 'right themselves in the end' if I kept calm about it all and pretended 'not to notice'. After all, she had been through this when I was a child, and I had reached 'maturity'. But I was the only one out of her ten with no desire for food and drink.

To make matters worse Chas always thoroughly enjoyed his

food, although his enjoyment was never complete unless he found something to criticise at meal-times. Possibly he felt I was concentrating on the children more than I did on him. He even used to remark that the tea I made for him was 'never twice alike' and resented my reply that to have made hundreds of pots of tea, and each one different, was quite an achievement. One Sunday morning at breakfast he was complaining that I hadn't cut the rinds off his bacon, even though it was cooked exactly as he liked. My mind and eyes were on the children. I had made theirs look so appetising with my prettiest plates, but they were not attempting to commence their breakfast. As I got up to get another plate from the sideboard, Chas was still complaining and as I passed him, I tapped him 'lightly' on the head with the plate and said, 'Oh, do stop complaining, for goodness sake!' Obviously I didn't know my own strength, for the plate broke over his head and as the pieces fell about his shoulders I beat a hasty retreat to the kitchen. 'Look out, Mum,' yelled Susan, and I glanced over my shoulder to see Chas, with a look of fiendish hate on his face and my beautiful cut-glass bowl in his hand. I ducked and the bowl hit the back door with a might crash. The bowl crashed into a thousand fragments on to the kitchen floor. At eye level on the thick wooden back door, where the glass bowl had made its impact, was a hollow tunnel. It had taken a piece of the door clean away.

As Chas gazed at it, his face white and worried, I felt suddenly sorry for him. We both knew 'what might have been' and then my thoughts were for the children. What effect would it have on them? What dreadful parents they had, they might remember it all their lives. I went back into the dining-room. Susan, pleased I wasn't coaxing her to eat, was reading a book. Little William was kneeling on a chair at the table with a look of excitement and delight on his face. In front of him he had lined up a vinegar bottle, a bottle of sauce, the cruet and a vase of flowers. 'More ammoonition, Mum,' he said to me in a tone of great happiness. Although, fortunately it hadn't affected the children, I knew then, that although Chas and I could argue happily until the cows came home, I must never ever lay my hands on his person again, however lightly, for both our sakes!

In 1952 my father's health began to fail. Perhaps his brain began to deteriorate before this. Chas would come home from football at Upton Park and find my father, a solitary figure, waiting for Clapton to resume play, the match having ended at least half an hour before. 'I can't understand why they only play for such a short time these days, they used to play until full time.' Gradually he became thin and finally was confined to bed. He was 90 so I suppose we should have expected it, but it was my first experience of real old age, he'd always been so active and alert. My mother was still spry and nursed him devotedly. My father had never really been close with Chas, indeed he had sometimes been quite unkind to him in little ways and although Chas had always been polite to my father he had never felt that fondness for him that I would have liked.

Now my father was failing, Chas was extra kind. In some way he began to feel great affection for my father, it was as though my father was *his* child. It was more than compassion for a helpless creature. Chas would shave and bath my father and give him a manicure. I did the shopping but sometimes on Saturdays Chas would get anything that was required. He would laugh to me at my mother's funny ways. She would ask perhaps for '1 lb of the best runner beans', etc. which Chas would get. She would inspect these and say to Chas, 'Were these the best quality?' 'Yes, Mum,' Chas would reply. Mother would then fetch her purse to pay Chas. 'How much were the beans?' she would ask. '4*d.* a lb.,' was Chas's reply, then Mother would look at the beans again and say, 'These are definitely not the best ones, I will only pay you 3*d.* a lb. for it is obvious to me they are the 3*d.* ones!' It was obvious Mother would brook no argument and Chas would always be the loser when doing any shopping for her. But he was too fond of her to argue, too grateful for what she had done for us all her life, and he was always amused by his encounters with her. Sometimes if I argued with him he would say, 'You are getting just like your mother, she always thinks she knows best.'

I imagined I would be with my mother and father until their lives ended, but something happened which altered the course of our lives. Robin was getting so very busy in his shop he suggested Chas went into the business with him. I was all for it for I liked being with Rob and Olive. There was an empty flat above their shop. Marjorie and her husband Alfred had purchased a tobacconists and confectioners opposite Rob's shop. It would be nice to be near them. The snag was that in Rob's shop there was no spare room for my parents. Chas was anxious to go, the future looked brighter then for a self-employed man. Winifred came to the rescue, as she always had done. She and her husband owned a village stores and post office in Berkshire. A red-brick building with plenty of room. Mother and Father would be welcome there. Mother of course would rather have stayed at Forest Gate, old people don't like change, but an ambulance was arranged for their journey to Winifred's, and I waved them good-bye. Mother gave me such a strange look as the driver closed the door and I went back into my house and sobbed. 'Don't cry, dear,' said Chas, 'you'll be able to visit your mother.' He didn't know my feelings of remorse that I had 'let Mother down'.

I was therefore delighted when Winifred invited us for Christmas. Christmas in the country seemed more blessed than Christmas in town, especially as snow was expected. A white Yuletide in Berkshire. It would be something for my children to remember, and preferable to the slushy streets of London. It was sad to know my father had left this world spiritually, for though he was there in that chintz-curtained room he knew no one, and reposed, a silent motionless figure, looking very small in the enormous four-poster bed. Mother, whose baby he had become, insisted he had a smile for her and he received tender care from us all. Father was in no pain. Mother was happy for she was needed.

The countryside, blanketed with sparkling snow, was breathtakingly beautiful. The children cut holly and mistletoe, excited to find it growing moist and fresh, not lying warm and limp on sale in the florists. We attended midnight service on Christmas Eve in the lovely village church and walked home in a glittering early dawn holding hands. Supper by the log fire, resin bubbling out of the freshly cut logs. We went happily to bed after filling the children's socks and pillowcases.

The next day the house was filled with guests. The turkey was, as always, the best we had ever tasted. The pudding allowed itself to be set alight without that damp squibbish struggle. In the evening we played all the Christmas games of our childhood and the house rang with laughter. Suddenly Mother said, 'Oh, Chas, my dear, what *is* the matter, what is troubling you?' We all gazed at my husband. His face was so very mournful. He looked ready for tears. Sadly he said, 'I was remembering my Christmas in the forces, when I was at Cap Matafou, Algiers.' He paused to let a large sigh escape while we all listened to hear a tale of utter tragedy. He took a brave deep breath and continued, 'We were given one tinned meat-pudding for two soldiers, one tinned fruit-pudding for two men, three tangerines apiece, and . . .' We waited breathlessly for his last front-line delicacy to be revealed. 'And,' continued a mournful Chas, '*six* sheets of toilet-paper instead of three.' Mass laughter filled the room like thunder, it shook the balloons and the paper lanterns. Explained Chas patiently, the laughter puzzling him in some strange way. 'The normal issue of toilet paper, was *three* sheets!' I could have hugged him with joy for I hadn't seen my mother laugh so spontaneously since my father became ill.

Lying in that lovely country bed that night, the sheets smelling sweetly of lavender, we held hands drowsy and happy. Chas said, 'Your family are so strange in many ways. They find amusement at such funny things!' 'What else?' I laughed as I closed my eyes. I dreamt of a giant Christmas-card. Not robins, or holly, or a manger scene, but Chas, dressed in the garb of a Puritan, the tall black hat, sombre clothes, and oh, such a down-cast face full of mournful reproach. The caption read, 'God rest ye merry, gentlemen'.